Love Yourself First: Creating a Foundation for the LYF You Desire

By Dr. Michael A. Wright

MAWMedia Group, LLC
Los Angeles|Reno|Nashville

Copyright © 2024 Dr. Michael A. Wright for MAWMedia Group, LLC

All rights reserved. No part of this publication may be reproduced, distributed, or transmitted in any form or by any means, including photocopying, recording, or other electronic or mechanical methods, without the prior written permission of the publisher, except in the case of brief quotations embodied in critical reviews and certain other noncommercial uses permitted by copyright law.

While we encourage the sharing of knowledge and the spread of ideas, we kindly request that all readers and users of this book respect the copyright owner's rights. Unauthorized reproduction, distribution, or transmission of any part of this book is strictly prohibited without prior written permission.

If you wish to use any material from this book for noncommercial purposes, such as in educational settings or for personal growth, please ensure that you provide proper attribution and adhere to fair use guidelines as defined by copyright law.

For permissions, inquiries, or any other related queries, please contact the publisher at

MAWMedia Group

www.mawmedia.com

ISBN: 978-1-943616-61-9

Contents

30-Day Love Yourself First Primer 7

Prologue 12
How We Discuss Mental Health and Self-Worth 13
    Clarifying the SELF 14
    Developing the SELF 19

Section I: Defining Love with Self in Mind 28

Chapter 1: Love in Actions (Active) 29
    PRINCIPLES OF ACTIVE LOVE 30
    IMPLEMENTATION OF ACTIVE LOVE 33
    ACTIVE LOVE COGNITIVE PRACTICE 35

Chapter 2: Saying "I Love You" (Verbal) 38
    PRINCIPLES OF VERBAL LOVE 39
    IMPLEMENTATION OF VERBAL LOVE 44
    VERBAL LOVE COGNITIVE PRACTICE 46

Chapter 3: Thinking I Love You (Thoughtful) .. 49
    PRINCIPLES OF THOUGHTFUL LOVE 49
    IMPLEMENTATION OF THOUGHTFUL LOVE . 53
    THOUGHTFUL LOVE COGNITIVE PRACTICE .. 56

Chapter 4: Love Under Pressure (Motivational) 59
    PRINCIPLES OF MOTIVATIONAL LOVE 60
    IMPLEMENTATION OF MOTIVATIONAL LOVE 64
    MOTIVATIONAL LOVE COGNITIVE PRACTICE 65

Chapter 5: Love in Good Faith (Inspirational) . 68
    PRINCIPLES OF INSPIRATIONAL LOVE 69
    IMPLEMENTATION OF INSPIRATIONAL LOVE 72

INSPIRATIONAL LOVE COGNITIVE PRACTICE 74

Section II: Love Practice 77

Chapter 6: Loving Yourself First 78

Chapter 7: Practice Love 90

Chapter 8: Becoming Love 99

Chapter 9: Being Love 107

Section III: Spiritual Abundance 114

Chapter 10: Introducing the Spiritual Plane .. 115

Chapter 11: Returning to God as Source 123

Chapter 12: Love from Abundance 131

Love Is by Dr. Michael A. Wright 139

30-Day Love Yourself First Primer

1: This is the month I invite you to love yourself better. Most of us think we love ourselves, but after an honest assessment, we realize that we could love ourselves better. If you learn to love You better, your love for others will be more satisfying to you and to those you love.

2: I recently realized a truth about love and a revelation about loving myself. Love is meant to flow from abundance, not apportioned like something you must earn. You will never run out of love or waste love when it comes from the overflow of love for yourself.

3: Do you love yourself? Are you patient with You or frustrated that you aren't further along? Are you kind to yourself or do you talk down, belittle, beat yourself up? These are just two areas that we fail in loving ourselves. Love never fails. Let's keep learning to love You.

4 Today begins the assessment. Love has 3 expressions and 2 contexts. Use them to assess whether your love for yourself is complete: Active, Verbal, and Thoughtful; Motivational and Inspirational.

5 Love is patient not rushed. Love is kind not rude. Love is generous not jealous. Love is humble not boastful or vain. Love is reasonable not defensive, honorable not gossipy, is considerate not obligated, civil not

angry, forgiving not blaming, temperate not reckless, and honest not deceitful.

6 Love protects instead of leveraging, trusts without disillusionment, hopeful not fatalistic, persevering not failing. Love never fails, but prophecies will fail. They will come to completion. Knowledge will be renewed with new information. (1 Corinthians 13: 4-8 Translation Based on KJV)

7 I am convinced that people think they love themselves but most 1) don't know what love is and/or 2) find contentment with an incomplete love. Loving yourself makes all relationships better. Some attachments must be released. But those that remain are transformative and progressive.

8 Loving yourself is more than being comfortable with what you see in the mirror. It is the ability to affirm You with the confirmation of your I AM. It looks like emotion management especially in the face of existential challenges. It is an act of creation not defense.

9 As with all creative acts, loving yourself begins with knowledge. That is the importance of the mirror exercise. You begin your self-love by sitting naked before a mirror, taking in what you see, accepting everything as it appears.

10 As your acceptance settles, your mirror reflects internally as well as externally. You begin to accept who, what, and how you are as the given that you begin your journey of self-love with. You are deserving. You are worthy. You are enough.

11 As you accept yourself, you recognize that your obligation is not to others, not ruled by flaws, judgments, or comparison. Your obligation is to You, to show up, to give your best, and to make your best contribution.

12 Judgment lingers, but it is self-assessment affirmatively answering the questions of your world. "Yes. I showed up. Yes. I gave my best.

Yes. I made my unique contribution." Against that evaluation, no negativity can prosper.

13 Understand that no one can give you a positive emotion or feeling that you are not able to give yourself. They shouldn't. You will always hear praise as incomplete. You will feel loved only up to a point. You will work incessantly never achieving satisfaction.

14 BUT, when you love yourself first, every relationship is an investment decision. "Do they deserve what I give?" rather than "I hope they receive what I can give?"

15 Your road to love yourself first suggests that you swim in the abundance of the love you create from within. Everyone gets splashed, but not everyone gets to swim with you.

16 Love Yourself First (LYF) isn't about priority. It is sequence. Love you before you attempt to share love with others. The love you create within will overflow to others. It will be pure, and it will be unconditional.

17 The Model of LYF is expression and context. It penetrates the ME working in the world (ROLE), the ME you know yourself to be (COMPETENCE), and the true ME inside (SELF) with authenticity, purpose, and consistency.

18 Active. Is the first expression of LYF. Actions speak louder than words. Actions communicate more than words alone. Patience accepts everything in its time. Kindness considers the capacity of the giver rather than holding unreasonable expectations. Forgiveness takes responsibility without listing an account of all the wrongs.

19 Verbal. Is the second expression of LYF. Spoken love is important to explaining your intentions. Humility speaks of love as reciprocity and mutual respect. Honor speaks love openly and complaints in confidence directly to the beloved. Spoken love remains civil through the stress of each conversation or disagreement.

20 Thoughtful. Is the third expression of LYF. Thoughts of love focus on openness and freedom rather than control. Thoughtful consideration is based on understanding and capacity not desperation from obligation. Thoughts of love center and calm allowing rest where recklessness may be tempting. Though held in the mind, love flows freely connecting with value from the inside out.

21 Motivational. Is the first context of LYF. Pressure reveals the character of love and pressure is more intense when you point the finger at yourself. Love faces the lessons with honesty. Refuse the inclination to belittle and put down. Protect your self-esteem while accepting that you have more to learn. This allows you to reason through the experience rather than defend against the growing pains.

22 Inspirational. Is the second context of LYF. Love in good faith hopes, trusts, and perseveres even when the evidence isn't obvious. Require your best and celebrate that effort. Love maintains the momentum of expectation not because it seems like it will work out but because you refuse to give in to fate. You are fearless because what we call a fail is just another steppingstone regardless of how bad it hurts.

23 Love Practice. You can't love others if you don't love yourself. You will always be in a position of attempting to connect and build something without having a store of it. Practice releasing yourself from requirements. Find that you are enough. Start here!

24 Your ambition and dissatisfaction with others comes from attempting to give them something that you fear wanting for yourself. Give yourself credit and space for continued growth. Fearlessly take YOUR next best step. Allow them to have their own journey. You too are competent and deserving.

25 You perceive your efforts as wasted because your love requires actions. The alternative is love given without expectation and without a sense of loss. Love yourself unconditionally and watch as self-

acceptance invites an abundance that spills over from you to others. You give from overflow rather than sacrifice.

26 Think in terms of love you give in return like to your grandmother. You don't feel like she should give it back to you in a certain way because she initiated it. You just enjoy it. Imagine if you could just enjoy the love you initiate inward and allow that to flow outward.

27 Spirit of Abundance. To be love is ability to rewrite your story from needing love from others to giving love freely out of your abundance. Love brings you into the spiritual plane (presence of god) where love is complete, resources are limitless, and all things are possible. Your overflow of love heals you more completely as you connect more deeply with the source of love.

28 Love changes you first. Love belongs to you first. Love becomes you first. You become love. You refuse abuse, mistreatment, and disrespect because you love yourself first. You are careful to allow and accept your feelings as real, valid, and honest for you. Return them to god to heal you holistically and renew your story each day.

29 Move from wait and wish to active creation of love as your lifestyle. Be love. Your love is not about discerning others or any concern for control of their actions. Those are concerns of the natural plane. The spiritual plane focuses on the fact that love energy draws like energy. You are free to continue in love.

30 The daily practice of becoming and being love is self-acceptance of You as complex. You are not required to be one thing or the other. You are complex and sometimes feel both sides and more. You can be brave and at the same time hold fear. You can be strong and simultaneously feel vulnerability. Accept You.

Prologue

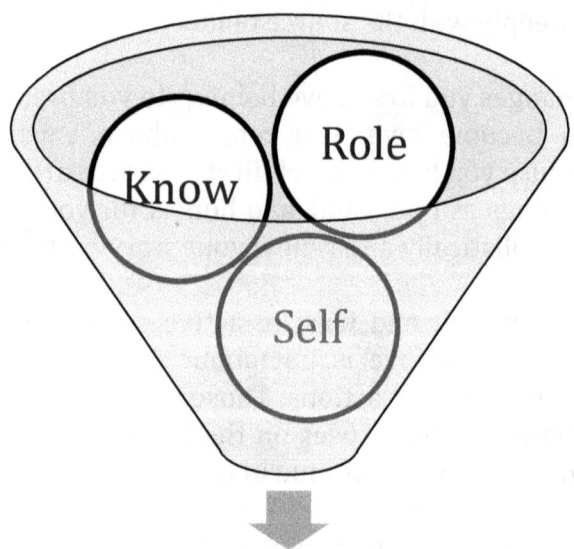

CONSTRUCTED ME

The Model of LYF is expression and context. If these were concentric circles, LYF penetrates the ME working in the world (ROLE), the ME you know yourself to be (COMPETENCE), and the true ME inside (SELF) with a revelation of identity, self-acceptance, and authenticity.

How We Discuss Mental Health and Self-Worth

Simply stated: When you love yourself, you experience life with more joy, passion, and success. You also construct boundaries that guard against those most damaging experiences that are under your control. Experiences that are out of your control can be processed for your good rather than allowed to limit your progress. The rest of this text intends to explain, in detail, HOW you love yourself first.

LYF is articulating your descriptions of self in more complex yet integrated ways expressing the importance and utility of each layer inner-self (SELF), self-knowledge (COMPETENCE), and observable self (ROLE). You are a complex and wonderful individual. The more you integrate and express You, the more any non-clinical anxiety, isolation, and self-loathing melt away like a thaw in Spring.

Self-esteem and self-worth are not simply about role. Concepts like self-esteem and others are almost always ROLE based when they are discussed. They are about choice at their core. You can choose high self-esteem. This is the determinate of your experience and activities as well as your definition of the inner SELF. COMPETENCE is your ability to bring information and ability to construct a You that you believe is worthy of respect, celebration, and love...True Love in action, word, thought, motivation, and inspiration.

LYF is an expansion of our understanding and expression of self-worth building upon a construct of mental health that is decidedly rooted in complex adaptive systems. Foregoing a lengthy explanation of the science, the point is simple: Your choices and effort create results that you can predict. The more you know about you, the more closely your predictions fit your outcomes. This means that you can directly increase your success or desired outcomes by increasing your self-knowledge. This is where the complexity comes in. You are more than just what you do, who you think you are, and who you hope to be. You are an integrated organism comprising all that and your interactions and interpretations with others. Your task is to support integration, increased options, sustainable effort, healthy interactions, and clear (unadulterated/unbiased/objective/accountable) interpretations. This defines self-worth and mental health.

Clarifying the SELF

> We cannot strive to be logical because we are emotional beings, but we can strive to always be practical. **Lamar Washington**

The world is full of people who do not know how to love themselves. They are stuck in a cycle of self-blame, shame, and guilt. Lack of self-awareness, self-efficacy, and autonomy keep people from truly loving themselves first. Many of us also simply did not receive a good model of loving ourselves. The people who were supposed to model for us instead gave us anxiety. Loving yourself first has the function of clarifying who you are. The clearer your expression of self, the more you invite what builds, complements, and enhances You. Repeat after me with the central question of clarifying self:

"What gives me LYF?"

Love Yourself First is abundant life founded upon the assumption that the universe is rigged in your favor. Love Yourself First (LYF) is not toxic positivity, arrogance, or unsustainable selfishness but an approach to feeling your emotions and sharing genuine empathy to You as an expression of character and self-esteem. It is identity, self-acceptance, and authenticity as a foundation or readiness for relationships and the knowledge that, if you are alone, you are in good company.

As you journey through the process of actively developing your self-love, consider the following objectives:

1. **Assess your current experience with self-love.** Understand where you are now, accepting your current state with open arms as the starting point of your journey.
2. **Identify a model for improving your relationship with Self (You).** Understand how self-love can act as a cornerstone for deeper, more fulfilling relationships with others.
3. **Implement techniques for self-celebration based on self-love and acceptance of You.** Apply practical methods of self-

love, from mindfulness practices to affirmations, to fuel your personal growth and satisfaction.

4. **Articulate a process for engaging with others through gratitude and abundance.** Learn how to share your overflowing love and abundance with others in a sustainable, enriching way.

To sustain LYF, keep this cyclical process at the forefront of your thoughts, actions, and intentions. Self-love is the starting point of an endless loop—a Jacob's ladder—spiraling upward towards greater personal growth, beautiful relationships, and a profound sense of peace and fulfillment.

Self-development in the context of LYF is a dynamic, multifaceted process that draws from different areas of being. These can be categorized into active, verbal, thoughtful, motivational, and inspirational components, each of which flows seamlessly with the definition of love central to LYF.

Active Self-Development: Action Speaking Louder

Where words may fail, actions step in to fill the void. Actions serve as concrete evidence of our commitments, including our commitment to love and nurture ourselves. Picture a day where you intentionally practice self-care, perhaps by preparing a healthy meal or setting aside time to unwind. These actions reveal your value for yourself, practicing love towards your body and mind.

Verbal Expression: The Power of Articulation

Verbal self-development involves expressing our intentions, affirmations, and aspirations out loud or in writing. Whether it's saying, "I love you" in the mirror or journaling about your personal growth journey, verbalizing self-love is a powerful method of making it real and tangible.

Thoughtful Self-Love: Deepening Capacity

Thoughtful self-love emphasizes the importance of deep understanding and the capacity for love, straying far from the path of desperation or obligation. Mindfulness exercises, meditation, and moments of reflection are the tools. The thoughts are open and giving centered upon your mind's capacity for understanding the self and cultivating love genuinely.

Motivational Growth: The Crucible of Character

The role of pressure in self-development cannot be understated. Enduring the pressure, while uncomfortable, reveals the discipline in our character and the depth of our love for ourselves. As we face challenges and hardship, our encouraging self-talk, purposeful resilience, and ever-improving ability prioritize our well-being and reflect genuine self-love in the face of adversity.

Inspirational Perseverance: Evidence of Faith

Self-love is rooted in self-development. Continuous development requires inspiration—a beacon of hope that encourages us to persevere, even when the evidence of progress isn't immediately obvious. Drawing from external sources of inspiration and tapping into our internal reservoirs of strength can fuel self-love and promote self-development.

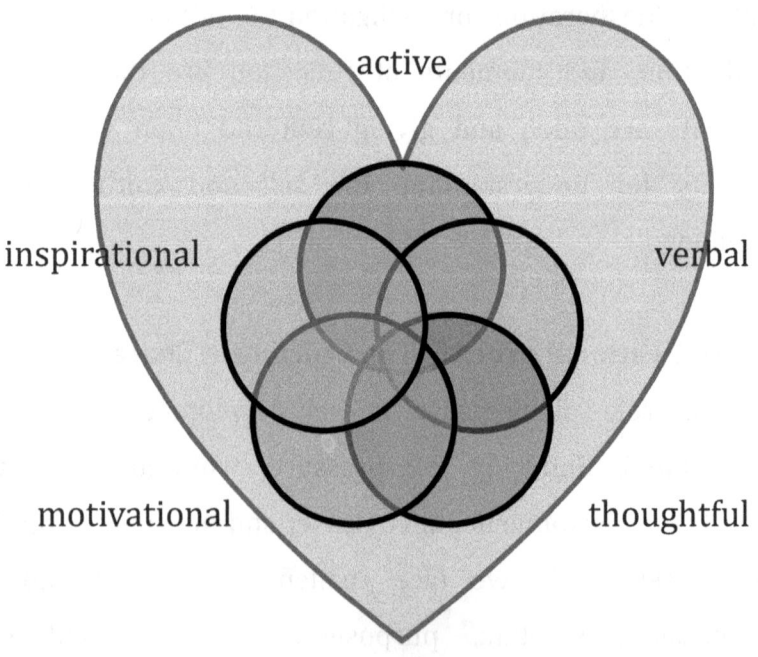

Developing the SELF

You must cultivate self-awareness, authenticity, and a deep understanding of your identity if you want to evolve as a human being. I am willing to argue with you because it's that important for you to accept this. I would rather not argue with you because I am confident that you will realize the utility of this statement at some point.

Most of us are trained early in life to review our goals and progress through the lens of our relationships with others. In the extremes, you could have unreasonably been required to make others happy, keep the peace, punish another, or keep another safe. You may have learned the unhealthy pattern of foregoing your development to ensure the security, safety, and respect of others. The result is that you think that adulting is a matter of security, safety, and respect for yourself. It is not only that.

Healthy adulting is self-development centered in identity, self-acceptance, and authenticity. This is what we call Character. Mastery of these enables You to create spaces of love and acceptance that you may choose to invite others into. You invite hoping for enhancement of the experience reciprocally based on what you know love does—motivate reciprocity. Consistency in your created space results in the reality of security, safety, and respect that you and others feel in that created space.

The central question of the development of self is,

"How do I sustain the LYF that is the created space of and for development?"

The answer is to Love Yourself First by prioritizing identity, self-acceptance, and authenticity on your journey that is creating, growing, and expanding your space. Take up more room in your life.

IDENTITY

Identity is a fundamental element of character development, and it plays a crucial role in the practice of Love Yourself First. Delve deep into your sense of self and gain a profound understanding of your identity.

Cultivate **Insight** into your strengths, weaknesses, passions, and purpose. This introspective process enables you to shape your character in a way that is developmental. Embrace the unique qualities and abilities that make you who you are, recognizing that they are integral to your character and have the potential to positively impact both yourself and those around you.

Integrity plays a vital role in affirming your identity. It requires acknowledging and embracing what you truly want, despite external influences or the opinions of others. Be honest about your desires, even in the face of misunderstanding, opposition, or feelings of unworthiness. You are not able to make decisions about change, integration, justification, or rationalization if you refuse to admit to the desires. By understanding and embracing this truth, you affirm your identity without judgement.

Empathy is another essential aspect of Loving Yourself First and shaping your identity. When it comes to prioritizing your well-being and happiness, it is critical to remember that your primary audience is not others, but yourself and the universe. Communicate your desires and aspirations confidently, even if others may not understand or agree. While it can be challenging to assert yourself, especially when someone else appears to hold control over the things you seek validation for, acknowledge that your power and favor extend beyond the constraints of time and external control. Give yourself the chance to be heard just as you would advocate for the chance for others.

SELF-ACCEPTANCE

Self-acceptance empowers you to embrace your truest self and find the beauty just as you do when you accept someone who you know has flaws. The flaws are not dealbreakers and character deficits. You see them for who they are like a road with filled potholes or a car with slight misalignment because of the potholes along the journey. Whichever analogy fits, you love yourself regardless.

Self-awareness is key to self-acceptance. Who you are is front and center in every discussion. Understanding forms the foundation for a meaningful relationship and a healthy relationship with You. Defend you. You are worthy of protection. You can do this in constructive and sustainable ways while also accepting accountability, being vulnerable, and maintaining integrity.

Self-Reflection. By taking the time to reflect on your expectations, thoughts, emotions, sensations, behaviors, and interpretations, you gain valuable insights into your patterns of thinking and challenge any limiting beliefs that may hinder your progress. This process of self-reflection allows you to cultivate self-awareness and make conscious choices that align with your values, paving the way for even greater self-acceptance.

Purpose plays a crucial role in self-acceptance. Embarking on the path of self-discovery requires a consideration of how you will develop as an individual in service to your purpose and in cooperation with others. People often talk about running from their calling. I reframe this as clarifying your calling and mechanisms. Accepting your calling and living as You (with a capital Y) is easier when you have a clear sense of what you are want to do, how you will do it, and who you BE even prior to the doing.

AUTHENTICITY

Authenticity is the practice of being true to yourself, living in alignment with your values, perspective, and self-definition. Being authentic involves the ability to correct the things about you that are out of alignment, the confidence to stand even when you are not supported, and to move beyond politeness to kindness rooted in honesty and timing.

Self-correction involves recognizing areas in your life where you may have compromised your authenticity and taking the necessary steps to adjust. This process requires self-reflection and honesty, as you assess whether your actions and choices align with who you truly are. By engaging in self-correction, you regain control over your choices and ensure that your words and actions truly reflect your essence and sustainably support your chosen path.

Confidence is another key element of authenticity. When you are confident in who you are, you approach interactions and progress with courage, positivity, and faith. However, confidence does not equate to naivety or blindly giving away your power. It is about engaging with others in good faith while discerning their energy and managing your energy in interactions. Confidence allows you to navigate relationships and goals with a sense of self-assurance and purpose.

Kindness is the third element that underscores authenticity. It extends beyond mere actions; it is a mindset and default position of genuinely wanting the best for others and promoting peace in the world. By embodying kindness, you recognize that your authenticity has the power to empower others to offer their genuine and compassionate presence to the world. Through these acts of kindness, you validate You and promote healthy spaces whenever you enter the room.

If this was not the pattern you learned growing up, you will need to evolve into a new approach to life that is LYF. The method of practice guiding your LYF is cognitive restructuring in six steps popularized by D. D. Burns in The Feeling Good Handbook.

- Step one: Identify the problem. It can be an event or trigger but isolate the origin of your emotional upset or dysregulation. Blame the persons at fault but take the responsibility to be the difference in this situation as respect for You.
- Step two: Articulate your emotions. Gather a set of words that are emotions and choose from among them to articulate **feelings** rather than situations, observations, or blame. Search the web for a list and choose what fits.

- Step three: Record your automatic thoughts. Pay careful attention to your sensations and anxious/motivating reactions in the moment of your emotion consideration. For each thought, rate the strength from 0=No Effect to 10=Catastrophic Effect (limiting your action/causing action).
- Step four: Analyze your automatic thoughts. Seek to admit, accept, and own the unrealistic, unfair, or irrational nature of your thoughts as expressed. The thoughts are what they are. You can make choices about what to do with them.
- Step five: Construct balanced thoughts through any number of intervention methods. David Burns offers 10 Ways to Untwist your Thinking. COACHMethod.com offers multiple systematic programs for processing through deconstruction and construction of healthy thoughts (Certain Way; Engaging Pain; BrainTrain; and other COACHMethod Interventions).
- Step six: Evaluate the restructuring process. Rate how strongly you agree with the Balanced Thoughts you created from 0=No Belief/Adoption to 10=Ultimate Freedom/Lowered Anxiety. Compare this score to the Anxious Thoughts rating from step 3. Explain the values in comparison to one another. Answer the following questions: 1) What would help to increase my score on the Balanced Thoughts Scale; 2) What would help to decrease my score on the Anxious Thoughts Scale?

Affirming One Love

Make no mistake, Love Is One. Love is and always will be. It is an energy that is never destroyed nor created. That is why its nature in the universe of things is hard to apply to ourselves. You know how to be, speak, consider, engage, and inspire others. But how do you give that energy to yourself? You first make the decision that love will flow from you. You next make a commitment to be love. Finally, you release love to its source. All the words that follow are a nature-based attempt to communicate a spiritual potentiality that we too often limit with our definitions, words, and attempts.

Yet, it is critically important that I make the attempt to illuminate a path with words because loving yourself first is a crucial step on the path to enlightenment for your highest experience. It is the only way that you can share in pure energy with others. To Love Yourself First means to joyfully engage when you're alone never agitated by time, enslaved by boredom, or coopted by your urges.

Time Agitation Replaced with Patient Non-Striving. You are not behind. That path only leads to disappointment from an unreasonable perfectionism. Patient non-striving is demonstrated when you choose to do what can be done rather than lamenting what cannot be done. It is an intentional focus on effort, process, and progress rather than deadlines, outcomes, and missed opportunities.

Boredom Replaced with Purpose. Purpose can look different on any given day. It is not about production or productivity every day. It is about listening to your whole self and responding with intentionality toward your clarified goals.

Health, well-being, satisfaction, fulfillment, and gratitude are a solid foundation. Face boredom with a ready set of activity including exercise, meditation, learning, serving, and giving. These will always produce more than the energy expended.

Urges Replaced with Inspirations. The most basic of urges are self-protection and sabotage. They are two sides of the same coin in your internal and interpersonal interactions. You build beyond these basic urges through experience and intentional learning. In its purest form, inspiration is a motivator beyond the basic urges. Inspiration connects experience and learning to form a direction for the energy you wield. As you feed your inspiration, you create satisfaction and fulfillment that you and others benefit from.

Section I: Defining Love with Self in Mind

Chapter 1: Love in Actions (Active)

LOVE IS AND IS NOT

Love is patient. not rushed.

Love is kind. not rude.

Love is forgiving. not blaming.

Love is often described as a verb because it requires ongoing action to maintain its presence effectively. This proactive approach is necessary for all relationships, including the ones we share with ourselves. When it comes to self-love, your job is one of consistent and intentional cultivation. As your self-love begins to thrive, you will feel more secure within You and create a positive impact on those around you.

Action speaks louder than words. This simple adage reminds us that actions are often more indicative of our intentions than any verbal expression. Our actions can reveal our dedication to nurturing self-love by indicating the steps we take to prioritize our well-being. Embracing this mindset can increase self-worth and help foster a healthy love for oneself.

PRINCIPLES OF ACTIVE LOVE

(Patience) *Patience embraces everything in its time. Patience is the capacity and the willingness to accept delay, difficulty, or annoyance without becoming angry or upset. Given to self, it feels like grace and progress at a steady pace.*

Let Go of The Little Things that often disrupt or strain relationships. Although minor issues, misunderstandings, or small annoyances may seem inconsequential, clinging to them can quickly escalate into larger problems. By cultivating the ability to let go and overlook these disruptions, you can maintain a harmonious bond with your loved ones, directing your focus towards what truly matters—love and understanding.

To foster a healthy and fulfilling relationship, it is crucial to maintain an open mind and encourage open communication when addressing these minor issues. By doing so, both you and your partner can concentrate on the bigger picture, fostering a deeper connection and shared growth. This approach establishes an environment where love, compassion, and understanding thrive.

Remember, patience does not mean ignoring or suppressing your emotions. It means recognizing that situations might not unfold as quickly or smoothly as desired and choosing not to let frustration overpower your actions and reactions. By embodying patience, you empower yourself to respond to challenges with grace and composure, ultimately fostering personal and relational growth.

(Kindness) *Kindness considers the capacity of the giver rather than holding unreasonable expectations. Kindness to oneself is treating ourselves with compassion and understanding, the same way we would treat a loved one. It's accepting our faults and mistakes and replacing self-criticism and judgement with self-nurture and care.*

Giving More Than You Take. Selflessness and a genuine desire to contribute to your partner's well-being and happiness are the hallmarks of such a relationship. This concept emphasizes prioritizing your partner's needs, providing emotional support, and engaging in acts of kindness without expecting anything in return. This selflessness fosters a loving and mutually supportive environment where both individuals can truly thrive.

Remember, love is an active endeavor. It goes beyond a passive feeling and requires your active engagement. Invest your time and effort in nurturing your relationships, understanding your partner's emotions, and maintaining open communication. By actively participating in the art of loving, you ensure that both individuals feel loved, appreciated, and understood. Together, you can navigate challenges, adapt, and grow as a couple, and foster mutual respect, trust, and understanding.

Embrace the power of kindness, selflessness, and active participation in your relationships. By doing so, you empower yourself to create a loving and fulfilling partnership, enriching both your life and the life of your partner. Remember, you hold the key to unlocking the immense potential within your relationships.

(Forgiveness) *Forgiveness takes responsibility without listing an account of all the wrongs. Self-forgiveness is about letting go of guilt and resentment towards oneself for past mistakes while remaining accountable for learning and more sustainable choices.*

Love Without Strings Attached. True love is unconditional, rooted in genuine admiration, respect, and empathy for another, without expectations, conditions, or hidden agendas. Loving someone without strings attached means accepting them in their entirety, embracing the flaws, and celebrating their unique qualities. It's providing support and care without any prerequisites or demands, offering a safe space where individuals can be their authentic selves. This unconditional love is the cornerstone of a genuinely loving and enduring relationship.

IMPLEMENTATION OF ACTIVE LOVE

Patient/Rushed

Patience teaches us that not everything happens instantaneously and that there is value in allowing time for events to unfold. It entails understanding that not everything is within our control, and sometimes, waiting and embracing the journey are key to a meaningful life. By being patient, we provide ourselves with opportunities to grow, heal, and develop. Contrarily, constantly rushing may lead to frustration, irritability, and overall dissatisfaction with our lives.

Adopting a patient mindset can help us better understand our emotions and needs while offering space for self-improvement. It reminds us that each step in our journey is just as important as the destination. Learning to savor these experiences and demonstrating patience toward ourselves ultimately strengthens our emotional resilience and self-love.

To love yourself, you must practice patience with your own growth and progress. It's important to remember that personal development doesn't happen overnight, it is a continuous journey.

For example, let's say you've set a goal to improve your physical fitness. You start working out, but after the first few weeks, you don't see any noticeable results and feel like giving up. Instead, demonstrating patience means persisting, understanding that meaningful change takes time, and it's part of the process. It could mean adjusting expectations, scheduling rest days, or varying routines to maintain motivation—all components demonstrating patience.

Kind/Rude

Kindness towards ourselves enables us to recognize our unique strengths and shortcomings without harsh judgment. It means offering acceptance and understanding of our limitations while celebrating the victories, however small they may seem. By treating ourselves with kindness, we make room for self-compassion and self-discovery.

On the other hand, a habit of harsh self-criticism and unreasonable expectations can lead to self-doubt, anxiety, and a diminished sense of self-worth. Maintaining an unkind attitude may prevent us from experiencing the true joys of personal growth and development. By replacing rudeness with kindness, we create a nurturing environment that allows self-love and self-appreciation to flourish.

Consider a situation where you make a mistake at work, and it leads to certain consequences. Practicing self-kindness doesn't mean overlooking mistakes, but it could mean reassessing your internal dialogue. Instead of harshly criticizing yourself thinking, "I'm incompetent, I ruined everything", applying kindness would look like acknowledging, "I made a mistake, it's a normal part of the learning process, next time I will approach differently."

Forgiving/Blaming

Practicing forgiveness toward ourselves requires being able to acknowledge our mistakes and failures without dwelling on them or blaming ourselves incessantly. It means taking responsibility for our actions, learning from them, and moving forward with grace. Forgiveness allows us to reevaluate our actions and behaviors without the burden of guilt or shame, ultimately empowering us to grow and change for the better.

Blame, on the other hand, can result in feelings of guilt, resentment, and self-loathing. This cycle of self-blame can inhibit personal growth and obstruct the development of self-love. By choosing to forgive ourselves, we embrace vulnerability and give ourselves the opportunity to change, heal, and love ourselves more profoundly.

For example, suppose you've had a friendship fall out due to a misunderstanding which escalated because of your own actions. You apologize, but the friend decides to end the relationship. It is natural to feel guilt and regret in such a scenario. Practicing self-forgiveness would involve acknowledging your actions, learning from them, and then letting go of the guilt and self-blame. It's about accepting you are human, you made a mistake, you have learned from it, and you will do better in the future.

ACTIVE LOVE COGNITIVE PRACTICE

Applying cognitive restructuring to patience, kindness, and forgiveness can help reframe negative thought patterns and cultivate self-love in a more profound way.

Patience

1. **Identify the problem**: You are losing patience with yourself because you're not making progress as quickly as you wanted.
2. **Articulate your emotions**: Frustrated, discouraged, restless.
3. **Record your automatic thoughts**: "I'll never achieve my goals", "I'm always failing."
4. **Analyze your automatic thoughts**: Understand the unrealistic nature of your thoughts and how impatience is contributing to the negativity.
5. **Construct balanced thoughts**: "Progress takes time, and I'm making an effort.", "I need to give myself space to grow and learn."
6. **Evaluate the restructuring process**: Assess how much you believe in the new balanced thoughts; work on increasing belief in them while decreasing your anxiety-based thoughts.

Kindness

1. **Identify the problem**: You're being unkind to yourself due to a mistake at work.
2. **Articulate your emotions**: Disappointed, ashamed, upset.
3. **Record your automatic thoughts**: "I'm always messing up.", "I'll never be good at this."
4. **Analyze your automatic thoughts**: Understand the irrationality of your thoughts and the lack of self-kindness in your self-talk.

5. **Construct balanced thoughts**: "People make mistakes, including me.", "I will learn from this experience and improve my skills."
6. **Evaluate the restructuring process**: Assess your beliefs in the new balanced thoughts; work on increasing those beliefs while decreasing anxiety-driven thoughts.

Forgiveness

1. **Identify the problem**: You're struggling with self-forgiveness after a friendship fall out due to your actions.
2. **Articulate your emotions**: Guilty, regretful, sad.
3. **Record your automatic thoughts**: "I'm a horrible person.", "I don't deserve friendships."
4. **Analyze your automatic thoughts**: Understand the irrationality of these thoughts and that they hold you back from self-forgiveness.
5. **Construct balanced thoughts**: "I made a mistake, but it doesn't make me a bad person.", "I can learn from this and work on building healthier relationships in the future."
6. **Evaluate the restructuring process**: Assess your beliefs in the new balanced thoughts, and continue working on increasing your belief in them while decreasing guilt- or anxiety-driven thoughts.

Chapter 2: Saying "I Love You" (Verbal)

LOVE IS AND IS NOT

Love is humble not boastful or vain.

Love is honorable not gossipy.

Love is civil not angry.

When words are said with love, they have the power to heal, uplift, and reassure. Just as action reveals love in doing, words express it by saying. A verbal acknowledgment of love combines the language of the heart and the mind to encompass elements of humility, honor, and civility. This chapter explores these three dimensions to help you navigate expressing love through words more effectively and mindfully.

PRINCIPLES OF VERBAL LOVE

Loving yourself involves the conscious choice of treating yourself with kindness, understanding, and respect. Implementing the values of Humility, Honor, and Civility into this process can magnify the effect of self-love. Let's explore each of these values separately with corresponding examples.

(Humility) *Humility is the mindful recognition of our limitations and acceptance of our flaws. It also includes celebrating our strengths without arrogance. Implementing humility in self-love means acknowledging that we have areas for growth and being willing to learn from our mistakes instead of condemning ourselves for them.*

For example, imagine you find that you are gifted in an area. You speak up to volunteer careful to articulate your strengths as well as the areas where you will need help. You engage a team that collaborates well with your skillset while supporting you to learn additional skills. This humble approach to self-love creates a space for personal growth and self-celebration.

Self-awareness is the conscious recognition and understanding of one's strengths, weaknesses, emotions, beliefs, and limitations. It plays a critical role in personal and professional development, paving the way for humility. By acknowledging our strengths, we can channel them effectively, while embracing our weaknesses opens the door for growth and self-improvement. Self-aware individuals recognize the limits of their knowledge and are open to the perspectives of others. This awareness fosters a healthy, balanced sense of self and prevents egotism. In turn, a humble approach facilitates better relationships, improved decision-making, and increased receptiveness to learning and feedback for continued self-improvement.

(Honor) *Honor refers to treating yourself with respect and integrity. It means being true to your values and principles, standing by them even when you're standing alone. By implementing honor in self-love, you show yourself the same level of respect and care that you would give to others, treating your feelings, thoughts, and experiences as valid and worthwhile.*

For example, treat yourself with honor by prioritizing self-care in your daily routine. If you are feeling overwhelmed with workload, honor your feelings and mental health. Instead of dismissing your stress and pushing through, take a break. Engaging in activities that relax you - like reading a book, taking a walk, or practicing yoga - is a practical way to do this. Honor your limits and prioritize your well-being over external demands.

In your pursuit of personal growth and fulfillment, it is crucial to turn your attention inward and embrace the dignity and respect you give yourself. By extending acts of kindness and understanding towards yourself, you can demonstrate and honor your own value and purpose.

When it comes to honor, it goes beyond recognizing and valuing the differences in others. It encompasses treating yourself with dignity, kindness, and understanding, regardless of your beliefs, background, or opinions. Just as you strive to create a culture of respect in your interactions with others, it is equally important to foster a culture of self-respect within yourself.

As you cultivate self-respect, you create an environment that is inclusive and harmonious, where you feel valued, accepted, and comfortable expressing your true self. This internal culture of respect empowers you to approach your personal and professional lives with authenticity and confidence. It provides a solid foundation for teamwork, cooperation, and productive communication, leading to your collective growth and success.

By recognizing the importance of turning your attention inward and extending acts of kindness and understanding towards yourself, you unlock the potential to cultivate a culture of self-respect. This, in turn, allows you to navigate your personal and professional journeys with authenticity, confidence, and a sense of purpose. Remember, embracing self-respect creates a strong foundation for healthy relationships, effective communication, and overall fulfillment. With the right guidance and support, you have the power within you to achieve your goals and live a life that reflects your true worth.

(Civility) *Civility involves being polite and respectful in your behavior and attitude towards yourself. As part of self-love, being civil to* *yourself means treating yourself kindly, especially during moments of mistakes or failures.*

For instance, when you're learning a new skill, there might be moments of struggle and perceived failure. You might feel tempted to berate yourself or quit, but practicing self-civility would mean encouraging yourself and treating the situation as a learning opportunity. Instead of saying "I am terrible at this. I should just give up," say to yourself: "This is harder than I thought it would be, but every expert was once a novice. I will get better with more practice."

In summary, Humility, Honor, and Civility can be important tools for practicing self-love. By acknowledging our flaws and potential (Humility), prioritizing our well-being (Honor), and treating ourselves gently (Civility), we can develop a healthier and more loving relationship with ourselves.

When it comes to treating yourself with civility as an act of "verbal love," it is essential to cultivate your internal voice and how you speak to yourself. To do this, two key themes emerge: openness to feedback and active listening. These themes, when applied to your relationship with yourself, can foster personal growth, effective communication, and a greater sense of self-worth.

Openness to feedback is a fundamental aspect of personal and professional development. By inviting constructive feedback and demonstrating a willingness to learn from others, you create an environment that values continuous learning, progress, and adaptability. Embracing criticism with humility allows you to reflect on your actions, identify areas for improvement, and foster a growth mindset. Instead of perceiving feedback as an attack, viewing it as an opportunity for growth and self-enhancement is crucial. This mindset promotes collaborative and cooperative relationships, where you can engage with others in an open and constructive manner.

Active listening is another powerful tool for cultivating a positive internal voice. Through active listening, you engage in careful and empathetic listening, seeking a deeper understanding of your own thoughts and emotions. This entails providing your full attention, using verbal and non-verbal cues, asking clarifying questions, and paraphrasing your own thoughts to confirm comprehension. Active listening not only fosters empathy but also enhances interpersonal connections and effective communication. By focusing on understanding yourself rather than immediately formulating a response, you create an environment within yourself where open and constructive dialogue can take place. This practice promotes self-reflection, problem-solving, conflict resolution, and fosters trust and rapport with yourself, underlining its significance in fostering civility and respectful self-relationships.

IMPLEMENTATION OF VERBAL LOVE

Humble/Boastful

Humility in communication cultivates an atmosphere of shared respect and reciprocity. It is a willingness to listen, to understand, and to appreciate without overshadowing or diminishing the other person's experience. This approach to speech fosters a deep connection, a resonance in dialogue that sings, "I love you".

On the other hand, excessive boasting can create a chasm of disconnect. While it's perfectly fine, even healthy, to be proud of one's achievements, constantly elevating oneself above others disrupts mutual respect, hinders reciprocity, and erodes intimacy.

For example, in expressing love, humility would sound like, "I really value and respect your perspective," or, "I learn so much from you." Conversely, a boastful statement may look like, "I always know better," or, "You don't understand things as well as I do." The humble approach acknowledges the other's contribution, reinforcing a loving bond, while the boastful approach may instill feelings of insignificance.

Honorable/Gossiping

Honor in conversations implies trust, respect, and integrity. Expressing love honorably means addressing grievances with the person involved directly and honestly. It involves communicating openly, even when it is difficult, and choosing words that dignify both parties involved.

Conversely, gossiping erodes trust, sows discord, and communicates a lack of respect. Talking behind someone's back, magnifying their faults or failures, or discussing their private matters with others, all fall under this category.

In the context of saying "I love you," being honorable would look like, "I have a concern that I would like to discuss with you," or, "I respect your privacy and would not discuss your personal matters without your consent." Gossiping, in contrast, involves breaking these codes of trust and respect, often leading to hurt feelings and broken relationships.

Civil/Angry

Maintaining civility is key to demonstrating love verbally, even during emotionally charged disagreements. Being civil doesn't mean suppressing anger but expressing it in a controlled, non-aggressive, and respectful manner.

Anger, when not managed well, can escalate to aggressive speech or behavior, hurting the feelings of the person on the other side. It can lead to things said in the heat of the moment that can't be taken back and may be regretted later.

Communicating love with civility could sound like, "I am upset because of this situation, but I want us to have a calm discussion about it." An angry and non-civil exchange may involve shouting, using harsh words, or making derogatory remarks.

VERBAL LOVE COGNITIVE PRACTICE

Loving oneself by implementing traits like humility, honor, and civility involves practicing self-reflection and self-regulation while maintaining respect and kindness towards oneself. Here's how it can be done:

Humility

Humility involves recognizing and accepting both your strengths and weaknesses without allowing ego to hinder your growth.

1. Identify the Problem: You have realized you're gifted in a certain area. However, you're hesitant to step up, given you also have areas that need support and improvement.
2. Articulate Your Emotions: You might be feeling eager to contribute, but apprehensive about appearing boastful or facing potential rejection.
3. Record Your Automatic Thoughts: "I might come across as showing off", "They could dismiss me because I lack certain skills".
4. Analyze Your Automatic Thoughts: Notice that the thoughts could stem from anxiety and self-doubt. Understand that everyone has strengths and areas for learning.
5. Construct Balanced Thoughts: "Recognizing my skills does not make me arrogant, and acknowledging areas where I need help

displays a willingness to learn. Constructive collaboration can bring out the best in the entire team."

6. Evaluate The Restructuring Process: Are the balanced thoughts generating a positive shift in perspective? Are they promoting a more proactive and collaborative approach? You could measure it by the level of comfort or confidence felt in taking initiative and working with the team.

Honor

Honor towards oneself means respecting yourself and your boundaries while maintaining integrity.

1. **Identify the problem**: You may be neglecting your own needs to please others.
2. **Articulate your emotions**: Exhausted, resentful, unhappy.
3. **Record your automatic thoughts**: "I will be a bad person if I say no", "I must always help others even at my own expense".
4. **Analyze your automatic thoughts**: Realize the unfairness of the thoughts and that self-care is important too.
5. **Construct balanced thoughts**: "It's okay to say no when I need to", "Taking care of my needs is not selfish, it's necessary".
6. **Evaluate the restructuring process**: Assess if the revised thoughts contribute to honoring yourself and your boundaries better.

Civility

To practice civility towards oneself involves treating yourself with kindness, respecting your own feelings, and finding peace even during challenging times.

1. **Identify the problem**: You might be overly critical and harsh with yourself.
2. **Articulate your emotions**: Frustration, disappointment.
3. **Record your automatic thoughts**: "I'm not good enough", "I always mess things up".
4. **Analyze your automatic thoughts**: Identify how these thoughts lack self-compassion and lead to self-deprecation.
5. **Construct balanced thoughts**: "I'm doing the best I can", "It's okay to make mistakes, they help me grow".
6. **Evaluate the restructuring process**: Evaluate if the balanced thoughts create more self-civility, leading to a kinder and more caring inner voice.

Chapter 3: Thinking I Love You (Thoughtful)

LOVE IS AND IS NOT
Love is considerate not obligated,
Love is temperate not reckless.
Love is generous not jealous.

Thoughts of love bring self-awareness, clarity, and a sense of harmony to our lives. When we think with love, we focus on openness, freedom, and understanding, rather than getting caught in a cycle of control, obligation, and self-criticism. By cultivating a loving mindset, we can navigate life's challenges with greater ease, embracing our strengths and weaknesses with humility and grace.

PRINCIPLES OF THOUGHTFUL LOVE

Self-love is an integral component of personal well-being. It manifests through various attributes, including consideration, temperance, and generosity. Each of these attributes plays a unique role in nurturing self-acceptance, respect, and nurturing growth. Let's delve into each one.

(Consideration) *Consideration in self-love entails being mindful of your needs—physically, mentally, and emotionally. Give thought to your actions in the context of authentic reflections and consider their potential impact on choices and the resulting well-being.*

Example: If you're stretched thin between work and personal life, considering your emotional health might involve marking out some "me-time" to disconnect, recharge, and regain balance. It could be as simple as taking a long walk, indulging in a good book, or practicing calming yoga sequences regularly.

Empathy, a critical component of thoughtful love, involves understanding and sharing another person's feelings. This capacity extends beyond mere sympathy, allowing us to deeply connect and empathize with what others are experiencing. Empathy requires active listening, open-mindedness, and a willingness to suspend judgment, requiring us to step outside our own perspectives to fully grasp the emotions of another person. Manifestations of empathy include expressions of understanding, validation of another's experiences, and conveying comfort or support steps. Empathy builds a robust and harmonious relationship, healing divides, fostering trust, and promoting open communication. It's the emotional glue that holds individuals together, cultivating deep emotional connections that form the foundation of a thriving, caring, and thoughtful bond of love.

(Temperance) *Temperance is the ability to maintain balance, moderation, and self-restraint. In self-love, it means making choices that foster long-term health and happiness, even when those choices demand patience and self-control.*

Example: Imagine you have an ambitious fitness goal. A temperate approach to this goal would involve crafting a balanced diet and a sustainable workout regimen rather than throwing yourself into a strenuous routine or adopting a harmful diet that promises quick results. It encourages patience and perseverance, understanding that true and lasting changes come with time.

Temperance cultivates moderation—a virtue necessary for maintaining balanced and healthy relationships. In the context of thoughtful love, moderation refers to regulating emotions, actions, and speech, ensuring that one's behaviors or responses do not escalate into harm or discord. For example, exhibiting restraint during disagreements demonstrates respect for the feelings and opinions of your significant other, preventing the escalation of conflict and reinforcing love and understanding. Moderation also involves disciplining personal desires and passions, ensuring that they don't overpower consideration for others' needs. This balance directly corresponds to peaceful and harmonious relationships, providing a nurturing environment for love to flourish thoughtfully and sustainably.

(Generosity) *Generosity in self-love isn't about giving material things to yourself. It's more about being generous with patience, understanding, and forgiveness towards yourself.*

Real short answer: Jealousy is what has you focusing on your flaws and unworthiness when you are more than flaws and worthy of everything good and perfect. It's limiting of your roles and resilience attempting to make you one-dimensional. [Perfectionism is a good example.]

The short version is to think to the two in comparison: generous or jealous. When you assess yourself, are you free with compliments and encouragement (generous) or do you withhold or focus on the negatives or what you need to fix (jealous)?

The longer answer has to do with how jealousy, possession, and control are judgmental attitudes with the goal of limiting and self-protecting. Being jealous of yourself is self-judgement (often unfairly) and limiting of your roles and resilience.

For example, you may say that you are not perfect, therefore you can't …whatever it is. Jealousy makes perfection the standard you must meet before you get rewarded. Generosity accepts that there is no requirement that must be met before you are deserving.

If you are working on a project at work, you may rather than focusing on the lack of resources and knowledge, construct your outline of tasks based on what materials you have, what you can secure, and the timeline you have. A generous approach would involve treating yourself with understanding, encouragement, and forgiveness. Show up and do your best. Accept that mistakes will happen. Use them as an opportunity for learning and growth rather than as a measure of your worth.

Integral to the concept of thoughtful love, selflessness signifies the generous act of prioritizing your loved ones' needs and wants over your own. It entails more than mere giving—it embodies the willingness to sacrifice time, energy, and resources for the happiness and well-being of the other person. A selfless individual extends support, patience, and kindness, even when their actions may bring inconvenience or sacrifice. They do not expect compensation, acknowledgement, or reciprocation, expressing love genuinely and authentically without any attached conditions. This attitude fosters a nurturing, respectful, and loving environment, strengthening mutual bonds and contributing to a relationship grounded in generous, thoughtful love. This is how selflessness is interwoven with the principle of generosity, enriching and deepening the very essence of love.

IMPLEMENTATION OF THOUGHTFUL LOVE

Considerate vs Obligated

When thinking lovingly, we consider others' feelings and well-being, ensuring our actions are considerate and respectful. However, it is important to distinguish between being genuinely considerate and acting out of a sense of obligation. True consideration arises from a heartfelt desire to uplift and encourage ourselves and others, while obligation creates mental barriers, fueling negative emotions such as guilt, resentment, and fear. By releasing ourselves from the shackles of obligation, we can flourish in a more compassionate, understanding, and loving way.

Temperate vs Reckless

In a world that sometimes glorifies impulsiveness and living on the edge, temperance and self-control can be underestimated virtues. When we think with love, we find a sense of balance, able to resist the temptation of reckless behavior. By embracing temperance, we can make wiser decisions and foster healthier relationships, not only with others but also with ourselves. We learn to cherish our minds and bodies by creating a nurturing environment, ensuring our actions align with our core values and promoting self-love.

Generous vs Jealous

A loving mindset invites us to be generous with our thoughts and emotions. Instead of harboring jealousy and self-doubt, focusing on our flaws or the success of others, we can cultivate a generous spirit, celebrating our unique gifts and rejoicing in the achievements of those around us. This generosity not only benefits others but also helps us become kinder, more compassionate individuals, deepening our connection with ourselves and the world at large.

Jealousy, on the other hand, confines us to a narrow view of our self-worth, trapping us in a cycle of negative self-talk and paralyzing us with self-imposed limitations. By letting go of jealousy and embracing generosity, we free ourselves from perfectionistic ideals, allowing us to experience the richness and beauty of our authentic selves.

The concept of grace lies at the heart of this approach. When we accept and understand the notion of grace, we learn to look at ourselves, and others, with an abundance of love and empathy. In the biblical context, the story of Lucifer reminds us that jealousy can lead to self-destructive behaviors and impede our capacity to recognize our inherent worthiness.

When assessing ourselves, it's essential to reflect on whether our thoughts are driven by generosity or jealousy. Do we celebrate our successes and accomplishments, or do we focus on our shortcomings and perceived failures? Adopting a generous, loving mindset allows us to recognize that we are worthy of love, happiness, and success, despite our imperfections. In doing so, we embrace our true purpose and the unique path that has been laid out for us.

THOUGHTFUL LOVE COGNITIVE PRACTICE

Applying cognitive restructuring to these three aspects of self-love can help reshape negative patterns, allowing for the development of a healthier, more accepting mindset. Here's how cognitive restructuring can be implemented:

Consideration
1. **Identify the Problem**: Neglecting your own needs and well-being due to a busy schedule.
2. **Articulate Your Emotions**: Overwhelmed, stressed, disconnected.
3. **Record Your Automatic Thoughts**: "I can't afford to take breaks," "My needs aren't as important as others' needs."
4. **Analyze Your Automatic Thoughts**: Recognize that these thoughts may be rooted in self-doubt and an exaggerated sense of responsibility.
5. **Construct Balanced Thoughts**: "It's essential to prioritize self-care, and taking breaks increases productivity and mental clarity."
6. **Evaluate The Restructuring Process**: Assess your belief in these balanced thoughts and your anxiety level around self-care.

Reflect on how embracing more self-considerate actions can positively impact your overall well-being.

Temperance

1. **Identify the Problem**: Struggling with impatience and a tendency to make impulsive decisions.
2. **Articulate Your Emotions**: Frustration, irritability, impatience.
3. **Record Your Automatic Thoughts**: "I must achieve my goals immediately," "Other people make progress faster than I do."
4. **Analyze Your Automatic Thoughts**: Acknowledge that these thoughts may stem from unrealistic expectations and comparisons to others.
5. **Construct Balanced Thoughts**: "Patiently working towards goals leads to lasting success. Everyone's journey is unique; comparing myself to others is unproductive."
6. **Evaluate The Restructuring Process**: Measure your belief in these balanced thoughts and your anxiety level around goal progression. Reflect on how practicing temperance can lead to a more balanced, fulfilling life.

Generosity

1. **Identify the Problem**: Struggling with a harsh inner critic and a lack of self-compassion.
2. **Articulate Your Emotions**: Inadequate, unworthy, self-condemning.

3. **Record Your Automatic Thoughts**: "I should never make mistakes," "I'm not good enough."
4. **Analyze Your Automatic Thoughts**: Understand that these thoughts come from self-judgment, perfectionist tendencies, and misconceptions about self-worth.
5. **Construct Balanced Thoughts**: "Mistakes are opportunities to learn," "I am deserving of kindness, understanding, and forgiveness."
6. **Evaluate The Restructuring Process**: Assess your belief in these balanced thoughts and your anxiety level concerning self-worth and self-forgiveness. Reflect on how cultivating an attitude of self-generosity can foster resilience and contentment.

Chapter 4: Love Under Pressure (Motivational)

LOVE IS AND IS NOT

Love is honest not deceitful.

Love is protecting not leveraging.

Love is reasonable not defensive.

Pressure has a unique way of revealing the true character of love, particularly when it comes to loving ourselves. In the face of life's challenges and setbacks, the way we respond to ourselves speaks volumes about our capacity for self-compassion and understanding. Learning to be honest, protective, and reasonable during these trying times allows us to foster personal growth while maintaining a healthy, loving relationship with our inner selves.

PRINCIPLES OF MOTIVATIONAL LOVE

(Honesty) *Honesty begins with truly understanding and embracing your feelings, emotions, strengths, and weaknesses. Living in your truth empowers you to stand confidently as you make your choices in life.*

In the pursuit of personal growth, the principle of honesty is instrumental in the journey of self-discovery. By acknowledging when you're feeling overworked and stressed, rather than brushing these feelings aside, you demonstrate a commitment to honesty with yourself.

For example, imagine you find yourself in a situation where you're feeling overwhelmed by work. Instead of ignoring or denying these feelings, honesty compels you to confront them head-on. You might say to yourself, "I need a break. Continually pushing myself at this pace will only harm my health. My wellness should be my priority." Honesty allows you to pave the path towards self-care, enabling you to establish boundaries and take the necessary rest that you need, rather than risking burnout.

To truly embrace the principle of honesty, it is essential to practice self-reflection. This involves honestly and truthfully acknowledging your feelings, emotions, and experiences. By facing your struggles with sincerity and openness, you create opportunities for growth and self-improvement.

Another aspect of honesty is being reasonable and accepting responsibility for your own journey. It's important to recognize that everyone's experiences and emotions are unique, and it is not your role to control or dictate the path of others. By focusing on your personal growth and desired outcomes, you empower yourself to take responsibility for your own actions and decisions.

Remember, honesty is the foundation of self-discovery and personal growth. By embracing honesty in self-reflection, facing your struggles with sincerity, and accepting responsibility for your own journey, you open the door to a world of authentic growth and self-empowerment. Through honesty, you can unlock your true potential and cultivate a life that aligns with your values and aspirations.

(Protecting) *Protecting ensures that you safeguard your mental and emotional health from negativity and harm. This is not immediate isolation or blocking. It is setting your filter and discernment to process interactions objectively.*

This means recognizing when certain relationships or environments pose a threat to your well-being and taking proactive steps to establish a positive and supportive space for yourself.

For instance, imagine you have a friend who consistently belittles your achievements and instills self-doubt within you. Instead of tolerating this behavior, it's crucial to protect yourself by setting clear boundaries and prioritizing your self-love and self-esteem. You might express, "While I appreciate our friendship, I need to surround myself with positivity and people who uplift me. My self-love and self-esteem are paramount, and I will not compromise them." This action not only safeguards your self-esteem, but also encourages self-love by ensuring that your environment fosters growth and development.

To fully embrace the principle of Protecting, it is essential to cultivate strategies that nurture a healthy balance between your emotional well-being, personal boundaries, and self-respect. This could involve creating boundaries in relationships, seeking support from positive and uplifting individuals, or engaging in activities that promote your overall well-being.

Additionally, practicing self-compassion is key. During challenging times, be gentle and kind to yourself. Recognize that setbacks and mistakes are natural parts of the human experience and essential for growth. By embracing self-compassion, you cultivate resilience, learn valuable lessons from your experiences, and continue moving forward towards personal growth and fulfillment.

Always remember that you possess the power and responsibility to protect yourself and maintain your emotional well-being. By prioritizing your self-esteem, setting healthy boundaries, and practicing self-compassion, you create a solid foundation of strength and resilience. Embrace the principle of Protecting, creating a nurturing environment that supports your growth and empowers you to unlock your fullest potential.

(Reason) *Reason encourages you to adopt a rational approach towards your self-perceptions and self-judgment. As self-love, this looks like accepting and tracing your motivations with respect and attentiveness.*

For example, let's say you experience failure in a new business venture. Instead of berating yourself and letting self-doubt creep in, use reason to analyze the situation objectively. Remind yourself, "Yes, the business may not have succeeded as I had hoped, but that doesn't mean I'm incompetent. Making mistakes and facing failures is a natural part of life. They do not define my worth or capability. I choose to see this as a valuable learning opportunity, not a reflection of my self-worth." This rational outlook promotes self-love by reinforcing the understanding that failures are not indicators of your worth or competence, and that learning from mistakes is an important part of your personal growth.

Remember to trust the process. Understand and accept that personal growth takes time and that challenges are a necessary part of the journey. Embrace these lessons with open arms rather than resisting them. By trusting in the process and embracing the lessons along the way, you empower yourself to unlock your true potential and discover the greatness that lies within you.

IMPLEMENTATION OF MOTIVATIONAL LOVE

Honest vs Deceitful

Honesty is the cornerstone of any loving relationship, and turning honesty towards ourselves is no exception. When we face difficulties, it is vital to confront our feelings with truthfulness and self-reflection, even if it feels uncomfortable. Being honest with ourselves involves acknowledging our emotions, strengths, and weaknesses without judgment or self-deceit.

When we are deceitful to ourselves, we avoid acknowledging our true feelings, undermine our potential, and minimize our achievements. This self-neglect leads to a growing emotional distance that hinders meaningful self-growth.

Protecting vs Leveraging

Under pressure, it is crucial that we protect our emotional well-being and self-esteem from negative self-talk and destructive thoughts. Safeguarding our self-love means building resilience and maintaining belief in our abilities, despite the challenges we face. To protect ourselves, we need to develop strategies that help us focus on positives, celebrate small accomplishments, and remind ourselves of our worth.

Unhealthy leveraging occurs when, instead of nurturing our self-esteem, we manipulate situations to justify negative actions or evade facing reality. This approach denies us the opportunity to learn from life's challenges and hampers the potential for personal development.

Reasonable vs Defensive

Facing life with a rational and reasonable outlook means having the wisdom to separate our emotions and experiences from those of others. We must accept responsibility for our actions while allowing others to have their own process. Understanding that each individual has their unique journey is essential for cultivating a loving relationship with oneself.

Defensiveness, on the other hand, is a barrier to growth. When we are constantly on the defensive, we refuse to accept our shortcomings and fail to make meaningful progress in our lives. Letting go of the need for control and perfection allows us to focus on the results of our personal growth and that of others.

MOTIVATIONAL LOVE COGNITIVE PRACTICE

Honesty

Problem: Feeling overworked and stressed

1. Identify the problem: Acknowledge the reality of your overworked condition and stress.
2. Articulate your emotions: Accept your feelings of exhaustion, stress, and possibly resentment.

3. Record your automatic thoughts: "I can't let anyone down. I must keep going."
4. Analyze your automatic thoughts: Realize that these thoughts are irrational, as personal health should always come first.
5. Construct balanced thoughts: "I can take a break. I must prioritize my health and well-being, and it's okay to say 'no' when needed."
6. Evaluate the restructuring process: Assess the shift in emotions and thoughts after aligning them with honesty towards your health and well-being.

Protecting

Problem: Negative friend who consistently belittles your achievements

1. Identify the problem: Recognize the harmful impact this friend has on your self-esteem and confidence.
2. Articulate your emotions: Understand feelings of hurt, annoyance, or frustration.
3. Record your automatic thoughts: "I should stick around. They might need someone."
4. Analyze your automatic thoughts: Accept that these thoughts might not be beneficial for your emotional well-being.
5. Construct balanced thoughts: "My emotional health matters. It's okay to distance myself from negativity to protect my self-love and confidence."

6. Evaluate the restructuring process: Gauge the shift in emotional state and thoughts after adapting them protectively for your well-being.

Reason

Problem: Failing in a new business venture

1. Identify the problem: Accept that the business did not succeed as initially planned.
2. Articulate your emotions: Recognize feelings of disappointment, sadness, or failure.
3. Record your automatic thoughts: "I am a failure. I can't do anything right."
4. Analyze your automatic thoughts: Realize these thoughts are irrational and unfair. Everyone experiences failures.
5. Construct balanced thoughts: "One failure doesn't define me. I will learn from this and improve for my next venture."
6. Evaluate the restructuring process: Measure the difference in emotional response and thought processes after introducing reasoned thinking.

Chapter 5: Love in Good Faith (Inspirational)

LOVE IS AND IS NOT

Love is trusting not disillusioned.

Love is hopeful not fatalistic.

Love is persevering not failing.

The journey of love, in many ways, is like walking through an uncharted territory. At times, the path appears illuminated and we tread with ease; however, shadows often obscure the way and challenge our resolve. It's during these uncertain periods that love practiced in good faith becomes pivotal. Love in good faith is trusting, hopeful, and persevering, even when clear evidence is lacking. It inspires us to demand our best, acknowledge the effort, and persist because we refuse to succumb to pessimism.

PRINCIPLES OF INSPIRATIONAL LOVE

(Trusting) *Trusting involves believing in your own abilities and potentials, building faith in yourself to take control of your destiny, and fostering a consistent, disciplined choice routine toward sustainability.*

By cultivating trust, you empower yourself to embrace new challenges, unlock your true potential, and achieve personal fulfillment. Consider the example of John, a team leader who delegates significant tasks to his team members for an important project. Although it may be tempting for John to oversee every detail, he chooses to trust in his team's abilities and believes that they can execute their tasks efficiently. John understands that trusting his team is not only crucial for their confidence but also essential for the overall success of the project. By placing trust in his team members, John fosters a positive and empowering environment that encourages growth, collaboration, and an outcome that surpasses expectations.

To apply the principle of Trusting in your own life, recognize your unique talents, skills, and potential. Believe in your ability to overcome challenges and achieve your goals. By building trust in yourself, you take control of your destiny and cultivate self-love, which fuels your personal growth and empowers you to reach new heights.

Take the first step today by embracing the principle of Trusting. Believe in yourself, foster self-love, and unlock the incredible power within you to create a life filled with purpose, success, and fulfillment.

Trust in your abilities and watch as you soar to new heights of personal growth and achievement.

(Hopeful) *Visualize a brighter future regardless of the current challenges and maintain a hopeful attitude to nourish your dreams.*

In the face of adversity, it is crucial to embrace the principle of Hopefulness. When Ashley was unexpectedly laid off from her job due to company downsizing, she initially felt lost and unsure about her future career prospects. However, Ashley made a conscious choice to remain hopeful. She firmly believed that this setback was actually an opportunity in disguise, presenting her with a chance to explore new career paths and unleash her potential.

Ashley actively nurtured hope by keeping a positive outlook and visualizing a brighter future, regardless of the current challenges she faced. She maintained a hopeful attitude, which fueled her determination to pursue her dreams. Ashley utilized her time wisely by brushing up on her skillset and networking within her desired industry. Her relentless hope paid off, as she eventually landed a job in a field she had always been interested in but had previously hesitated to explore.

To apply the principle of Hopefulness in your own life, strive to cultivate a positive outlook and maintain a hopeful attitude. Even during difficult times, visualize a brighter future and believe in the potential for growth and success. Remember that setbacks are often steppingstones to something better. Foster hope, nurture your dreams, and fearlessly embrace new opportunities. By embodying the spirit of Hopefulness, you empower yourself to overcome challenges and unlock your true potential.

(Persevering) *Investing the time, dedication, and unwavering determination to learn, practice, and grow and achieve remarkable growth.*

In your quest for personal growth and self-discovery, the principle of Persevering plays a pivotal role. Take inspiration from Thomas, who faced numerous failures during his attempts to learn the guitar. Initially, he contemplated giving up, feeling disheartened by the challenges of mastering instrumental music. However, Thomas consciously decided to persevere, understanding that learning something new requires time, dedication, and unwavering determination. He acknowledged that giving up would only result in inevitable failure.

By embodying the spirit of perseverance, Thomas committed to constant practice, patience, and motivation. With each passing day, his guitar skills gradually improved, serving as a testament to the strength of his perseverance. Thomas embraced each struggle as a steppingstone in his journey, using his failures as a catalyst for growth. He understood that every stumble presented an opportunity to rise even stronger.

To apply the principle of Persevering in your own life, adopt a determined mindset. Embrace the struggles you face along your path, recognizing that they are valuable learning opportunities. Instead of giving in to discouragement, view setbacks as steppingstones toward personal growth and success. Maintain unwavering determination, constantly pushing yourself forward. By persevering, you will unlock your true potential and achieve remarkable growth.

Remember, each challenge you encounter is an opportunity to unveil your resilience and strength. Embrace the principle of Persevering, and let each stumble become a catalyst for greatness. Stay determined, keep moving forward, and witness yourself rise stronger than ever before. Your journey of personal growth is within your reach—embrace the power of perseverance and unlock your boundless potential.

IMPLEMENTATION OF INSPIRATIONAL LOVE

Trusting vs Disillusioned

Trust is the backbone of love in good faith. Trusting yourself means standing tall in the face of doubt, nurturing a steadfast belief in your abilities and potentials. It means acknowledging your own power to shape your destiny, rather than being manipulated by external circumstances. Trust fosters resilience and courage, fueling the determination to forge ahead even during the challenging moments.

On the contrary, a sense of disillusionment weakens the bond of self-love. When we are disillusioned, negative self-talk overpowers our thoughts, clouding our mind with doubts, fears, and insecurities. With a poisoned mindset, the rays of hope and faith struggle to shine through the darkness.

Hopeful vs Fatalistic

Fueled by a deep trust in oneself and a positive outlook, hope is another cornerstone of love in good faith. Hope infuses our life with optimism, helping us visualize a bright future even when current circumstances seem daunting. Embracing hope means viewing obstacles as mere temporal setbacks on our journey, not fatal roadblocks ending our pursuit of growth and fulfillment.

Conversely, a fatalistic approach towards life starves our dreams of their potential. When we adopt a fatalistic mindset, we accept defeat before the battle has even begun, clipping the wings of our dreams and ambitions with the shackles of despair.

Persevering vs Failing

The ultimate manifestation of love practiced in good faith is perseverance. A persevering spirit harnesses the power of trust and hope to maintain momentum, even in life's most stormy waters. By persevering, we assert our refusal to bow down to adversity, transforming each stumble into a steppingstone that propels us higher in our journey toward self-love and acceptance.

Contrarily, interpreting challenges and setbacks as failures leads to feelings of inadequacy and self-doubt. Seeing failure as an end rather than part of the journey impedes self-growth and faith.

INSPIRATIONAL LOVE COGNITIVE PRACTICE

Trusting

Problem: Doubt your abilities while overseeing a significant project.

1. Identify the problem: Recognize the lack of trust your capabilities.
2. Articulate your emotions: Understand feelings of anxiety, apprehension, or control.
3. Record your automatic thoughts: "I won't handle this well without obsessing over it or waiting until the last minute motivated by pressure."
4. Analyze your automatic thoughts: Reframe your sense of scarcity and fear of failure to reveal learning opportunities.
5. Construct balanced thoughts: "I am competent and continually learning. I will schedule consistent, informed, systematic work and make my contribution. I will learn something valuable no matter the outcome."

6. Evaluate the restructuring process: Measure the alteration in attitudes/confidence levels after restructuring thought processes to instill trust.

Hopeful

Problem: Loss of a job and uncertainty about future opportunities.
1. Identify the problem: I feel barriers to acceptance of job loss and fear its implications.
2. Articulate your emotions: Recognize feelings of fear, worry, or frustration.
3. Record your automatic thoughts: "I won't find another job as good as the last one."
4. Analyze your automatic thoughts: Deconstruct the negative and pessimistic nature of these thoughts.
5. Construct balanced thoughts: "Job loss is a setback, but it also provides a chance to explore new opportunities. I am skilled and I have hope for the future."
6. Evaluate the restructuring process: Gauge the emotional change and thought recalibration after adapting a hopeful and positive outlook.

Persevering

Problem: Struggling to learn to play the guitar and feeling like giving up.

1. Identify the problem: Acknowledge difficulty in learning the guitar.
2. Articulate your emotions: Grasp feelings of frustration, disappointment, or impatience.
3. Record your automatic thoughts: "I am not good at this. I should just stop trying."
4. Analyze your automatic thoughts: Admit the defeatist nature of these thoughts.
5. Construct balanced thoughts: "Learning is a process that requires patience and perseverance. I will continue practicing and improve with time."
6. Evaluate the restructuring process: Evaluate the shift in feelings and thinking patterns after incorporating perseverance.

Section II: Love Practice

Chapter 6: Loving Yourself First

The first step towards any kind of growth begins with self-awareness — knowing who you are. This starting point becomes the bedrock upon which we build all the other aspects of our lives, especially relationships. The most significant of these relationships is the one with Yourself. This endeavor of self-discovery is a personal journey that commences with exploring the depths of our psyche. A journey of introspection, also known as self-reflection, and self-awareness.

The Self-Awareness Learning Curve
It's crucial to comprehend that prioritizing oneself is not an act of narcissism but rather a sign of self-love. Only you can genuinely understand, feel, and cater to your unique needs. There is no one else on the face of this Earth who has had your exact set of experiences, who possesses your individual skills, or who can offer the world the

exclusive 'you' factor. We are all irreplaceable and invaluable because of our unique identities. There is no other being that can stand as a proxy for you, be it in your professional or personal life.

Understanding and acknowledging your uniqueness does not imply egocentricity. Rather, it's about loving yourself enough to know and accept your path in life—sometimes this might lead to making decisions that might not be in line with others' conveniences. Being oblivious to our own needs and wants often leads us on a path of self-neglect and engenders resentment for individuals who unwittingly pricked our feelings along the way.

Self-love and knowledge about oneself form the cornerstone for nurturing and loving others. It also provides confidence and authenticity needed to find and fulfill your purpose. The essence of purpose sprouts from self-love—it is the genesis of all beginnings. A clear understanding of the self: who you are, your values, your preferable way of life, and the reason why—facilitates sharing that clarity with others in a sincerely authentic way.

When we are thrown into the gray zone of self-doubt or confusion about these aspects, we can find ourselves in uncomfortable situations. Our inefficiency to effectively express our inner-most feelings and beliefs can lead to embarrassing encounters, or it can establish a fear of unpleasant reactions from others, thus initiating a silence offering advice that isn't intrinsic to our beliefs. Such advice often translates into echoing opinions extracted from someone else's thought space —

a mediocre blog that they might have stumbled upon and decided to absorb and later share.

Healthy association with others entails autonomy, not a reactionary impulse set off by an approaching relationship or an emotional bond. You don't erect walls to isolate yourself, but rather to preserve your sanity and your peace. Building healthy boundaries are all about nurturing your genuine self and fostering resilience to withstand conformity, chaos, and complacency.

Your boundaries should be reflective of many factors, such as the equal give-and-take in relationships; a balance between what can be done and what should be refrained from; the priority of catering to your happiness before focusing on another's happiness.

Authenticity Reflections

As humans, many of us are held captive to a socially conditioned notion - we ought to mold ourselves into someone different from who we truly are for the sake of earning approval or rewards such as raises, promotions, recognition, etc. We unknowingly lose sight of our genuine selves as we become dependent on external factors for our self-worth. This dependency leads us down a path where our identity is contingent on societal accolades rather than our core selves. Eventually, this drives us further away from authenticity and closer to conforming to societal expectations or rules that may not resonate with our deepest desires.

Immersed deeply in these illusions of success, countless individuals spend their lives simply going through the motions - doing what's expected of them without stopping to question or scrutinize anything. They fail to invest time in understanding their true selves or their personal aspirations. They miss out on asking themselves crucial questions such as: What do I want? Who do I want to be? What dreams define the vision of my life five, ten, twenty, or forty years down the line?

Engaging with oneself openly and honestly becomes an awkward proposition, and this lack of honesty leads to problems in interaction with others. Without a strong sense of self, honest communication with others often feels like a daunting task. You worry about whether they will accept you rather than standing confidently knowing that your tribe will see and celebrate you.

Lack of self-awareness, confidence, and autonomy are significant barriers preventing individuals from truly loving themselves. Authentic self-love is difficult when you lack knowledge about your own self. If you lack faith in your abilities and potential, self-love seems unattainable.

This is where the significance of habits comes into play. They act like a scaffolding that supports us in our journey of becoming more self-aware and confident. In essence, self-love is a journey marked by a better understanding of your values and beliefs—and eventually living in alignment with them.

Loving yourself first is a testament to your purpose and intention to honor who you are. They form a significant part of our daily habits and routine. Ask the questions:

1. Who do my actions say I am?
2. What do I value?
3. What do I need to feel fulfilled?
4. What routine fits my desired lifestyle and production aspirations?

Love Is Applied to Yourself First

Acts of self-love like prioritizing time for rest and relaxation are indeed gestures of self-love rather than overindulging in compulsive work habits or sacrificing sleep for tedious working hours in a job without passion. These acts, while seemingly small, are crucial. They help conserve energy so that when unexpected situations or emergencies arise, we have ample reserves at our disposal to prevent burnout. Through purpose and intention, we each hold the blueprint for self-love inside us. Remember, you are the architect of your own life..

Sadly, much of the world is designed by individuals who haven't learned to love themselves first or understand their core values and needs. Their life 'architecture' is faulty because they built expansive plans without erecting a strong foundation. How much can be expected from someone about love, care, and understanding when they themselves lack self-love? Another's lack of self-compassion and understanding should never be the yardstick for us.

Loving yourself first is a transformative journey that encompasses various aspects of personal growth and development. Each area contributes to the foundation of self-love, empowering individuals to cultivate a genuine, compassionate relationship with themselves. Let us explore these love areas and their significance in fostering self-awareness, autonomy, boundaries, and authenticity with examples.

Active Self-Development: Speaking Louder through Action

Actions speak volumes, showcasing our commitment to self-love and nurturing. Imagine a day where you deliberately practice self-care, such as preparing a nourishing meal or setting aside time to relax. These actions demonstrate your value for yourself, a resounding affirmation of love for your body and mind.

- Prioritizing regular physical exercise to promote overall well-being and self-care.
- Engaging in a hobby or activity that brings joy and fulfillment, allowing yourself time for personal enjoyment and growth.
- Listing and inviting meaningful goals that align with your passions and values, fostering a sense of purpose and accomplishment.

Verbal Expression: The Power of Articulation

Verbal self-development involves expressing our intentions, affirmations, and aspirations through spoken or written words. It could be as simple as looking into the mirror and saying, "I love you" or journaling about your personal growth journey. Verbalizing self-love in these ways makes it tangible and real, reinforcing your commitment to yourself.

- Engaging in positive self-talk and affirmations to cultivate a healthy and encouraging internal dialogue.
- Writing a gratitude journal, expressing appreciation for the positive aspects of your life and recognizing your own worth.
- Sharing your story or experiences with trusted individuals or in a supportive community, allowing your voice to be heard and validated.

Thoughtful Self-Love: Deepening Understanding and Capacity

Thoughtful self-love goes beyond desperation or obligation. It emphasizes the importance of deep understanding and the capacity for love. Engaging in mindfulness exercises, meditation, and moments of reflection are tools that nurture your mind's ability to genuinely understand and cultivate self-love.

- Practicing self-compassion by acknowledging and accepting your imperfections, embracing yourself with kindness and understanding.

- Engaging in self-reflection through journaling or meditation, creating space to understand your emotions, thoughts, and needs.
- Investing time in learning and personal growth, whether through reading self-help books, attending workshops, or seeking guidance from a coach or mentor.

Motivational Growth: The Crucible of Character

Pressure plays a significant role in self-development, revealing the depth of our character and love for ourselves. As we face challenges and adversity, our encouraging self-talk, purposeful resilience, and continuously improving abilities prioritize our well-being. This self-compassionate response reflects genuine self-love even in the face of difficult circumstances.

- Setting and enforcing healthy boundaries in relationships and commitments, valuing your well-being and protecting your energy.
- Celebrating your achievements and milestones, recognizing and nurturing your own personal growth and progress.
- Embracing resilience and self-belief in the face of challenges, viewing setbacks as opportunities for learning and growth.

Inspirational Perseverance: Evidence of Faith

Self-love is rooted in self-development, and perpetual growth requires inspiration. It serves as a beacon of hope, propelling us forward even when progress seems elusive. Drawing inspiration from external sources or tapping into our internal reservoirs of strength fuels our journey towards nurturing deeper self-love.

- Surrounding yourself with inspiring and supportive people, seeking role models who uplift and motivate you on your journey.
- Engaging in self-care practices that restore and rejuvenate your mind, body, and spirit, such as taking regular breaks, practicing mindfulness, or indulging in activities that bring you joy.
- Finding moments of solitude and reflection to connect with your inner self, allowing for self-discovery and nurturing a stronger sense of authenticity.

Romance, Relationships, and Loving Yourself First

Loving yourself first is not a checkbox exercise that you complete in anticipation of a potential relationship or attachment to someone else. It is a lifelong practice that enhances every aspect of an individual's well-being and does not specifically pertain to romantic connections.

When you love yourself first, it stems from a place of true inner happiness and contentment, which allows for an authentic, healthier, and more fulfilling relationship with another person.

Understandably, it's disappointing and hurtful to realize that your partner may not be able to love themselves, making it difficult for them to be fully available to love and support you. However, it's crucial to remember that you are not in the wrong for wanting to be in a relationship where both individuals value self-love and practice it consistently.

Having an ideal image of what a perfect partner might look like does not make you wrong either. It's natural to have certain standards and expectations, which can guide you in finding someone who aligns with your values. The person you choose as your romantic partner has the freedom to come close to your criteria or may very well be different altogether, which doesn't make them any less deserving of love. But their inability to meet every criterion on your list does not necessarily mean they are the wrong person.

Loving yourself first is not a morally right or wrong action. It is neutral in its essence, and anyone can practice it. Although self-love is not always simple or easy, its practice benefits your well-being and allows your best self to shine through.

When both partners in a relationship understand and value the principle of self-love, they create a solid foundation for their partnership, built on mutual respect and understanding. This foundation enables their connection to become stronger, more profound, and withstand the test of time.

Below are a few reasons why self-love is essential in romantic relationships:
1. It fosters healthy communication: People who practice self-love are better equipped to express their needs, feelings, and expectations openly and honestly, leading to healthier communication between partners.
2. It reduces co-dependency: Loving oneself first ensures that each person functions as an independent individual, reducing the chances of co-dependency and unnecessary pressure on their partner.
3. It increases empathy and support: A healthy level of self-love helps you to be more empathetic and understanding of your partner's emotions and needs, creating more emotional balance within the relationship.
4. It lessens the chances of emotional burnout: By giving yourself the care and love you deserve; you recharge and revitalize your emotional batteries. This allows you to continue giving love and support to your partner without becoming emotionally drained.
5. It contributes to personal growth: Loving yourself first can encourage you and your partner to keep growing as individuals – emotionally, mentally, and spiritually. This growth can create a stronger bond in the relationship as you both evolve together.

Loving yourself first is essential for establishing a healthy and satisfying romantic relationship. It is not a reaction to a potential romantic connection or an emotional attachment; it is an ongoing, rewarding practice that improves your overall well-being. Although it has no moral value, self-love plays a pivotal role in the dynamics of a romantic partnership by fostering healthy communication, reducing co-dependency, enabling personal growth, and providing a solid foundation on which partners can build a strong, lasting connection.

Chapter 7: Practice Love

True love, or One Love, begins with appreciating and valuing You in actions, words, thoughts, motivation, and inspiration. Before you can sustainably love others, you must first learn to love You. It's a You-First proposition. Let's address your dissatisfaction with the world—a proxy for your dissatisfaction with You. After that, we can discuss the Certain Way you can nurture self-love.

You Alone Are Worthy

You alone are worthy. When you practice self-love and release yourself from self-imposed requirements, you uncover the inherent worth that resides within. It is crucial to recognize that your worthiness extends from your being as a human being. You have the power to choose what you will BE.

You deserve every good thing that life has to offer. Remember that karma operates throughout the universe, and what you put out into the world will come back to you. By intentionally shaping your reality, aligning your actions with your desires, and making your unique contributions to the world, you will receive what you truly deserve.

You are enough, just as you are. It is not about what you do, but about embracing who you are and making decisions based on that truth. Your worthiness is not determined by external factors or societal expectations. Acknowledge and embrace your enough-ness in the present moment, free from the pressures of seeking validation from others.

This is your journey of self-discovery and growth. You have the power to unlock your own value and potential. Embrace the empowering truth that you are worthy, deserving, and enough. Trust yourself and let this realization guide you to a path of self-love and personal fulfillment. The choices you make and the actions you take will shape your journey towards unlocking your true potential. Remember, you can cultivate a deep and compassionate love for yourself, paving the way for a life filled with purpose and authenticity. Let your worthiness shine and embrace the limitless possibilities that await you.

Dissatisfaction: The Root and Remedy

Yet, you may be bogged down in the pressures of life extending from poor patterns and negativity that you have incorporated into your self-talk. As a defense, this often manifest as criticism of others. You can gauge how much work you need by the level of awareness about how critical you are. The more you deny accountability for your criticism, the more work you need to mind your purpose.

Our dissatisfaction with others stems from unaddressed fears and unfulfilled desires within ourselves. When we attempt to give love to others without addressing our own needs, our ambition can inadvertently cause friction in our relationships. To rectify this situation, give yourself credit and the space for continued growth. Embrace your competence and worthiness, and fearlessly take your next best step towards personal development. By doing so, you empower yourself to build more nurturing and understanding relationships, while also allowing others to traverse their own unique journeys. This admonishes the abundance of love represented in the varied backgrounds and experiences of those around us. They may not always mesh well with your experience, but the prosocial variety is always to be celebrated.

We learn to see love as an abundant, overflowing resource, rather than a limited commodity tied to specific actions. Through this transformation, we create space for meaningful connections, personal growth, and an abundance of love that reaches out to others and enriches the world around us. You can accomplish this remedy to dissatisfaction as follows:

Balance giving and requiring. The challenge lies in finding the balance between giving and requiring in our relationships.

Occasionally, our desire to give to others is outweighed by the fear of our own failure. To overcome this, identify your vision and take decisive action towards realizing it. Embrace the knowledge that you never truly fail if you continue to move forward, learn from your experiences, and invest in personal growth.

Love is more than Transactions. Love is a Route to Being as a prerequisite to enlightenment. Avoid the transactional view of love – thinking of love as reciprocation or a return on investment. Instead, love should be seen as a consistent effort to be the best version of oneself, irrespective of the partner's attributes. The primary focus should be on cultivating your genuine self unapologetically, fostering individual growth and self-love.

Overcoming the Perception of Wasted Efforts. The perception of wasted effort often stems from a belief that love must be accompanied by specific actions. True love is experienced freely, without expecting anything in return and without feeling any sense of loss. By loving yourself unconditionally and fostering self-acceptance, you create an abundance of love that naturally spills over into your relationships with others. You don't own love. You are not giving love; you are sharing in the experience of love.

Love Without Expectation. The key to genuine relationships lies in cultivating the ability to give love freely, without reservation or expectation. Consider the love shared between you and your grandmother. You do not expect her love to be returned in a particular way simply because she initiated it. Instead, you enjoy the love she offers and reciprocate it just as freely. This mutual appreciation and unconditional affection create strong, lasting bonds that enrich both of your lives.

Understanding Love: Self-Love and the 'Certain Way'

When we typically conceptualize love, the emotion we experience tends to focus on the needs satisfied and the emotional fulfilment gained from another person. Yet, as the dynamics of the relationship change over time, we may feel that our love is incomplete or inconsistent. To navigate this ebb and flow of emotions, we must introspect and evolve our understanding of love with a focus on self-love. That is, Love Yourself First. We can be more certain in the process by following the 'Certain Way' as outlined by Dr Michael A. Wright. In this changed perception of love, not everyone may connect with you or reciprocate your feelings, and that's okay. True connections, after all, happen with those who value themselves and appreciate your experience of self-love enough to share in it with you.

Two crucial tenets form the basis of this evolved approach to love - being a benefit to others and transforming fear and uncertainty into committed endeavors. To push beyond the initial stumbling blocks of fear and uncertainty, Wright's Certain Way provides five potent tenants: thought, belief, faith, gratitude, and will.

Thought. By channeling and focusing your thoughts on a clear vision of what you want, you allow yourself the opportunity to dream, aspire, and design your best life. When you align your thoughts with your true desires and passions, you nurture self-love by prioritizing your well-being and happiness.

Belief. When you believe in your infinite potential and embrace the concept of boundless opportunities provided by the universe, you show yourself love by acknowledging your self-worth. This mindset empowers you to make bold choices and strive for your goals without limitations or fear of inadequacy.

Faith. Cultivating faith in your ability to achieve your desires allows you to live in the present moment and appreciate your current state. By radiating positivity and joy as you live your life, you nourish self-love and enhance your capacity to take on challenges and grow.

Gratitude. Expressing gratitude for your place in the universe, your unique purpose, and the power within you fosters a deep appreciation for your life and experiences. This acknowledgment strengthens your connection with the universe and promotes self-love by embracing your value as an individual.

Will. By taking proactive steps towards achieving your goals, guided by your understanding and trust in your vision, you demonstrate self-love through dedication and perseverance. Overcoming uncertainties and focusing on one step at a time shows that you prioritize personal growth and invest time and energy in yourself. This approach changes the narrative of love from being a 'commodity' to a 'state of being'.

By consistently practicing thought clarity, belief, faith, gratitude, and will-power, you can push through barriers like fear and uncertainty. These practices will guide you from a sense of lacking towards flourishing in abundance, where love is not merely 'enough' but is overflowing.

When Change is Warranted

The Love Yourself First (LYF) program empowers you to uncover the layers of your inner-self, self-knowledge, and observable self. It teaches you the importance of embracing each aspect of yourself and the utility it brings to your life. When you love yourself, amazing transformations occur. You experience life with joy, passion, and success. Self-esteem and self-worth are not just about the roles you play, but about the choices you make.

When we talk about change, it's not about completely altering who you are at your core. Instead, it's about embracing honesty and being true to yourself. When you are authentic, connected with your desires, and guided by values that promote kindness, there is no need for drastic changes. The key lies in finding integration and harmony between your inner self and the external pressures you may face.

Now, you may be wondering: how can you navigate the expectations and pressures that society places on you without compromising your true self? How do you stay internally integrated and continue to express yourself authentically in the face of external influences?

It starts with boldness and unapologetically recognizing the unique contributions you have to offer the world. Embracing this truth requires a deep sense of self-awareness. Take the time to reflect on your values, desires, and purpose. Understand who you are at your core and what truly matters to you. This introspection becomes the foundation for your journey of self-integration and self-expression.

Your truth may require courage, resilience, and an unwavering belief in your own worth. This itself is a transformation. As you embark on this transformative process, identify the areas of yourself that you feel called to change. However, always remember that the act of change should come from a place of love and self-acceptance, not from a desire to conform or please others. When change is rooted in authenticity and kindness towards yourself, it leads to evolution through learning rather than disjointed starts and stops.

Approach change with curiosity and openness. Embrace growth and seize opportunities for self-improvement, knowing that it reflects your commitment to becoming the best version of yourself. Set clear goals and develop actionable steps to make progress towards those changes. Celebrate each milestone along the way, reinforcing the positive impact your choices are having on your life.

Throughout this process, remember that you hold the power to shape your own narrative. Express yourself boldly, unapologetically, and authentically, knowing that your unique contributions are valuable and deserving of recognition. Embrace your strengths and areas of growth, always clarifying your contribution and the meaningful impact you make in the world.

Love Yourself First is not a stagnant state of being, but a continuous journey of personal empowerment. It serves as a reminder that you are worthy of love and that your voice matters. Embrace the power of honesty, integration, and self-contribution. Love yourself enough to nurture your authentic self and engage in acts of self-improvement that align with your values and desires. If this is the change, the change is warranted.

Chapter 8: Becoming Love

Maturity: The Quest for Self-Understanding and Self-Love

Embarking on the journey of maturity begins with acknowledging and embracing your individuality, appreciating the value of your personal attributes and capabilities, and recognizing your inherent worthiness of love.

Never underestimate the power of intentional language. By consciously choosing your words and expressing positive affirmations and aphorisms, you create intentional spaces that shape your self-perception and foster self-love. Speak words of kindness, encouragement, and empowerment to reinforce your sense of self-worth and nurture a loving relationship with yourself.

Thoughtful self-love involves the ability to distinguish, discriminate, discern, and deconstruct. These cognitive processes contribute to your personal growth, integration, and evolution. Engaging in self-reflection and self-awareness allows you to identify unhealthy patterns of thinking and challenge any limiting beliefs that hinder your progress. Through practical exercises and strategies, you can actively engage in thoughtful self-love and cultivate a more authentic and fulfilling life.

Take the time to cultivate positivity in your thoughts, actions, and environments, as it can have a profound impact on your self-talk and self-love. Adopt a positive mindset and seek out healthier spaces to create a foundation of motivation that fuels your personal growth and fosters a loving relationship with yourself. I will provide you with motivational tips and techniques that empower you to overcome challenges and maintain a positive outlook on your journey towards maturity.

The path to self-understanding and self-love may not always be easy, but by persisting through hardships and setbacks, you will emerge stronger and more capable of creating love in your life. Actively work towards nurturing love in your life. This encourages you to take proactive steps towards your own happiness and fulfillment.

Engage in a media diet of stories individuals who have persevered and created love in their lives. These stories serve as reminders that maturity is an ongoing journey, and with your determination and self-compassion, you can achieve a deep sense of self-understanding and self-love.

The Practice: Cultivating Love Through Self-Expression and Gratitude

In the journey of self-love, every aspect of your life—your actions, words, thoughts, and emotions—is permeated by this essential practice. To truly love yourself, it is crucial to fully embrace your inherent worth and value, not only in moments of triumph but also during the struggles and everything in between.

When faced with challenges or consumed by self-doubt, remind yourself to approach these moments with love, openness, and gratitude. Whether you encounter failure, uncertainty, overwhelm, or inconsistency, each of these experiences presents valuable opportunities for growth and self-improvement. Instead of succumbing to negative self-talk or denying yourself credit for your efforts, choose to respond with love and appreciation. Recognize these challenges as chances to grow, learn, and evolve into a better version of yourself.

One powerful way to express self-love is through the art of self-expression. Allow yourself the freedom to express your true thoughts, feelings, and desires without judgment or fear of rejection. Whether it's through creative outlets like writing, painting, or music, or simply by speaking your truth and asserting your authentic self, self-expression can be profoundly liberating and contribute to a greater sense of self-love.

In the face of adversity or self-doubt, it can be easy to lose sight of the blessings that surround you. Practicing gratitude is a transformative tool that can help shift your perspective from scarcity to abundance. Take a moment each day to count your blessings, whether big or small, and truly appreciate the positive aspects of your life. By focusing on the abundance that exists, you cultivate a mindset of appreciation and attract more positivity into your life.

Additionally, leveraging gratitude to overcome fears can be incredibly empowering. When you approach your fears with a grateful heart, you create a space of courage and resilience. By acknowledging and appreciating the lessons that your fears offer, you can transform them into opportunities for growth and self-discovery. Embrace gratitude as a powerful tool on your journey to self-love and watch as it enables you to embrace challenges with a newfound sense of confidence and strength.

To incorporate self-love into our daily lives, consider these practices:

- **Listen**: Be attentive to your thoughts, feelings, and bodily sensations. Acknowledge and honor your emotions without judgment and give yourself permission to experience them fully.
- **Open to the answers**: Be receptive to the guidance and wisdom within you. Trust your inner voice and intuition to reveal the best course of action or next steps on your journey of self-growth.
- **Give yourself credit**: Celebrate your successes and achievements, no matter how small they may seem. Acknowledge your accomplishments and the effort you've put

into your personal growth journey. Recognize your resilience and perseverance.

- **Respond with love**: Treat yourself with kindness, compassion, and understanding, even during times of struggle or disappointment. We all make mistakes and have setbacks, but these moments provide opportunities for growth and self-improvement.
- **Practice gratitude**: Cultivate a grateful mindset for the experiences—both positive and negative—that you encounter in your life. Appreciate the lessons they teach and the opportunities they provide for self-discovery and personal growth.

Practicing self-love means expressing love for oneself in thought, word, and action, under all circumstances. Embracing each experience with love and gratitude creates a positive, nurturing environment for personal growth and paves the way for deeper, more meaningful relationships with others. By continually practicing self-love and appreciation, you strengthen your connection with your inner self and expand your capacity to share love with others.

The Character of Love Beyond Possession

As discussed in the Prologue, healthy adulting is centered in character development, which involves nurturing self-awareness, embracing one's identity, and cultivating authenticity. By mastering these aspects, we create spaces of love and acceptance that welcome others into our lives. Rather than seeking possessions or demanding reciprocity, we invite others to share in our experiences and enhance them through genuine connection and collaboration. This shift in mindset allows us to move away from transactional relationships and towards more fulfilling and meaningful connections even without requiring it explicitly.

From an early age, many of us are taught to evaluate our goals and progress through the lens of our relationships with others. Unfortunately, this can lead to the unhealthy pattern of prioritizing the happiness, peace, or safety of others over our own personal development. We may have learned to sacrifice our growth to ensure the security, safety, and respect of others. The notion of possessing self-love or seeking love from external sources can hinder our personal development. The result is that we approach our self-love as a possession akin to ensuring security, safety, and respect for ourselves.

Focusing on possession in relationships leads to problematic dynamics. Possession in our relationship with ourselves is also problematic. When we love ourselves first and embrace self-love as character development, we open ourselves up to new possibilities. Instead of focusing on possessing self-love, which suggests a limited resource, we shift our mindset towards creating space for the expression and experience of love. This involves cultivating a sense of openness and enjoying our experiences without expectation or attachment. By doing so, we create an environment where love can naturally flow enhancing our relationships and our personal growth.

Consistency is a key factor in creating spaces of love and acceptance. When we consistently foster a mindset of openness, authenticity, and self-development, we create a reality of security, safety, and respect. Others will feel this genuine sense of security and be drawn to the spaces we have cultivated.

Interdependence. The experience of being loved dramatically expands and deepens when it intertwines with another's self-love. The encounter becomes a celebration of individuality, validation of self-love, and a reinforcement of one's inherent worthiness. It's about two individuals—each complete and self-sufficient—choosing to share their individual completeness with one another thereby making the collective experience even more enriching.

This level of maturity in love moves away from dependency and embraces interdependence. It fosters mutual respect, shared growth, lasting understanding, and deep connections. Far from the tumultuous rollercoaster of emotions commonly associated with romantic love, mature love is serene, stable, resilient, and utterly profound.

Maturity in the context of love is not merely about growing older or accumulating experiences. It's about developing a profound understanding of one's self-worth, cultivating self-love, and being open to the idea of sharing, rather than seeking, love. This character enriching personal development is central to the practice of love. The understanding that you are worthy of love, and that this love comes best from within you, sets the foundation for healthier relationships and a more fulfilling life.

Gratitude is the powerful practice of expressing yourself authentically, counting your blessings, and leveraging its transformative energy to overcome fears. It is the art of acknowledging and appreciating the abundance that exists in your life, allowing you to shift your perspective from scarcity to abundance. Through gratitude, you cultivate a mindset of appreciation, empowering yourself to face challenges with courage and resilience.

Chapter 9: Being Love

In the pursuit of love and understanding, it is crucial to remember that love does not equate to allowing others to mistreat or disrespect us. A firm belief in the universal deservedness of respect and kindness should form the cornerstone of the way we approach ourselves and others.

Universal deservedness is the LYF approach to being love. This is as opposed to unconditional love. Unconditional love is not always the most sustainable approach. A mother's love extends no matter what choices her child makes. As a child of a father who could have made better choices, I was always haunted by the allowances my grandmother gave my father. Her unconditional love gave him license and kept him protected from the consequences of his behaviors. It is conjecture to assume that failing would have taught him lessons that would have taken route, but it is undeniable to assert that my grandmother's attentions and energy would have been better spent on other endeavors.

I remember she famously borrowed $400 from multiple people to bail him out of jail. He had been picked up on an outstanding warrant for unpaid child support. Foregoing the obvious fact that she felt a responsibility for her son and a satisfaction in looking after him, that money could have gone to other obligations.

Yet my father deserved love. Being love with universal deservedness would have tempered my grandmother's responses toward less responsibility for reaction and more responsibility for proactivity. She may have required him to pay rent holding a portion of his earnings for his child support obligations. She may have provided information and encouragement for him to plan before those financial obligations became legal entanglements. She may have instilled in him a love for himself prior to his engagement of women who made the choice with him to conceive of children amid their chaotic relationships. Being love would mean communicating a standard, setting boundaries, and allowing the results of informed choices.

The Point of Clarity: Being Love vs. Being a Doormat

In the journey of Love Yourself First (LYF), it is important to recognize the distinction between being love and being a doormat. Being love does not mean remaining silent in the face of disrespect or unkindness. On the contrary, it is about standing up for oneself with grace and assertiveness, without resorting to anger or animosity. At the core of this approach lies an unwavering belief in the inherent value and worth of all individuals, including ourselves. We are all equally deserving of respectful and loving treatment - anything less is simply not acceptable.

In the context of #LYF, being love means setting clear boundaries and asserting our worth. It is about recognizing that we have the right to be treated with kindness and respect, and taking proactive steps to ensure that this is honored in our interactions with others. Setting boundaries is an act of self-love and self-care, a way to protect our well-being and maintain a healthy sense of self.

However, it's important to note that being love does not entail harboring negative emotions or holding onto resentment towards those who disrespect us. In the context of #LYF, being love means practicing understanding, forgiveness, and centeredness. It involves recognizing that every individual, including ourselves, is deserving of love and respect. It is about approaching situations with empathy and compassion, seeking to understand the motivations and struggles of others. This does not mean excusing or tolerating disrespectful behavior, but rather responding from a place of love and asserting our boundaries without compromising our own well-being.

By embracing the principles of being love in #LYF, we honor ourselves and others. We recognize that our worth is not determined by the actions or opinions of others, but rather by our own inherent value. It gives us the strength and courage to stand up for ourselves while maintaining a sense of integrity and compassion. It is through this approach that we can navigate challenging situations and foster healthy, loving relationships both with ourselves and with others.

Being love is a powerful expression of self-empowerment and personal growth, and it is at the heart of the Love Yourself First journey.

The Discussion: Love vs. Mistreatment

In the journey of Love Yourself First (LYF), it is crucial to engage in internal dialogue that centers around understanding and fostering respect in conversations about love versus mistreatment. These discussions should prioritize a deep understanding of the other person's perspective, guided by empathy and compassion. It is not about reacting emotionally, but rather about sharing emotions and engaging in reasoned discussions that promote mutual understanding and growth.

During these interactions, it is essential to practice active and attentive listening. Approach the conversation with the same level of care and respect that you would give to someone you truly value and appreciate. By truly listening, you create an environment that encourages open and honest communication. It sets the stage for a dialogue that is founded on respect and understanding.

As you engage in these conversations, let love be your guiding principle. Choose to respond from a place of love, even when faced with mistreatment or disrespect. This does not mean condoning or accepting inappropriate behavior, but rather responding with grace, empathy, and compassion. By doing so, you can create space for growth, mutual understanding, and resolution.

Remember to aim for a dialogue that is open, honest, and respectful. This involves expressing your thoughts and emotions in a constructive manner, while also giving the other person the opportunity to share their own perspective. Approach the conversation with an open mind, willing to consider alternative viewpoints. By fostering an environment of respect and compassion, you create the foundation for healthy, meaningful discussions.

Throughout this process, keep in mind the importance of self-care and self-respect. Recognize your own worth and ensure that you are setting healthy boundaries in these conversations. If the dialogue becomes toxic or unproductive, it may be necessary to step away and prioritize your well-being.

By engaging in internal dialogue that centers around understanding and fostering respect, you not only contribute to your personal growth but also foster healthier and more compassionate interactions with others. Remember, you have the power to shape the conversations you engage in and to approach them with love, respect, and an unwavering commitment to self-empowerment and personal growth.

Letting Go: Recognize When to Part Ways

In your journey of personal growth and self-discovery, it is imperative to recognize when it is time to let go of unhealthy or detrimental relationships. Not all relationships are beneficial or conducive to your well-being, and parting ways can become an act of self-love and preservation. Remember, letting go does not diminish your capacity to love; rather, it is a conscious acknowledgment of incompatibility or the realization that the current situation is not supporting your mental, emotional, or spiritual well-being.

When a relationship reaches its end, it creates a spacious canvas for growth and presents opportunities for all parties involved to lead more rewarding and fulfilling lives. Although letting go can be challenging, it often becomes an essential step for personal growth and overall well-being. It provides you with the opportunity to redirect your energy towards building a life that aligns with your values and nurtures your soul. Embrace this process of letting go as a transformative journey that can offer valuable insights into your own desires and aspirations.

As you navigate the path of personal growth and self-discovery after parting ways with a relationship, focus on developing your capacity to love and understand from the inside out. Engage in deep self-reflection and introspection, exploring your desires, boundaries, and values to cultivate a profound connection with yourself. This self-awareness and understanding will empower you to form healthier and more fulfilling connections with others in the future.

Being love encompasses not only having open and respectful conversations but also recognizing when it is time to let go if a relationship becomes unhealthy or disrespectful. By practicing love in this manner, you create a sacred space for meaningful connections, personal growth, and an abundance of love that not only enriches your life but also reaches out to others. Always remember, you possess the power to choose relationships that align with your well-being and to create a life that is filled with love and fulfillment. Trust yourself to recognize when it is time to let go and embrace the endless possibilities for growth and self-discovery that lie ahead.

Section III: Spiritual Abundance

Chapter 10: Introducing the Spiritual Plane

God of Our Fathers: Perceive Love as the True Divine Essence

When we talk about God, our perspectives are often shaped by various personal and cultural beliefs, understandings, and portrayals. This perception, however, may inhibit our ability to experience God in His entirety. Wording that includes "the universe" or "higher power" seek to expand our view and vocabulary about what we are describing.

Observing, testing, and verifying occurrences in the natural world is a systematic process that allows us to gain a deeper understanding of how the world works. It is through this process that we can uncover truths about our reality and expand our knowledge. To observe, we must engage our senses and pay close attention to the details and patterns that emerge. By doing so, we can gather objective data and evidence.

Once we have gathered data through observation, the next step is testing. Testing involves designing experiments or procedures to investigate specific phenomena and gather additional evidence. This process allows us to isolate variables, control conditions, and collect quantitative and qualitative data. Through rigorous testing, we can verify the accuracy and consistency of our observations, ensuring that they hold true under different circumstances.

However, as we delve into the realm of spirituality, we move beyond what can be solely observed, tested, and verified in the natural world. Spirituality invites us to consider the plane of higher existence or a broader sense of God, transcending the confines of the empirical and physical realm. It goes beyond what can be measured and quantified.

When interpreting natural phenomena through a spiritual lens, we approach them with faith, hope, and positive expectation. We recognize that there are aspects of the world that surpass our understanding and incorporate elements of mystery and wonder. With faith, we trust in a higher power or a divine presence that guides and influences our experiences. Hope allows us to cultivate optimism and anticipation for what lies beyond our current knowledge. Positive expectation encourages us to believe in the infinite possibilities for growth, connection, and transformation.

By combining our empirical observations with spiritual interpretation, we can form a more holistic understanding of the world. This integration allows us to embrace both the tangible and the intangible, appreciating the depth and complexity of our existence. It reminds us that while we may not have all the answers, our faithful perception can guide us towards a greater appreciation of the mysteries and interconnectedness of life.

Viewing a God of Love

The essence of God surpasses human attributes typically associated with Him beyond the roles of a father or a friend. To perceive God in a more all-encompassing way, you may want to visualize God as the highest form of love—unconditional, all-embracing, and ever-present. When we view God in this light (pun intended), we begin to comprehend the essence of divine love. We begin to understand that love is not just a feeling—it's a state of being, it's the divine essence that permeates all creation. It is the unifying force that is one and completes us all drawing us into that oneness.

In contemplating the essence of God, let us adopt a broader perspective that challenges us to expand our understanding. This view invites us to recognize God as the ultimate creator, orchestrator, author, and finisher. Seeing God through this lens encourages us to embrace the power of love and acknowledge that creation itself is our birthright, granting us the ability to cultivate our own creativity.

The concept of orchestration reminds us that within the confines of nature and its laws, we are granted a noble dominion over our own lives. It signifies our rightful place in the intricate web of existence, enabling us to navigate our journey with purpose and intention. By recognizing this authority, we gain the freedom to make choices aligned with our values and aspirations.

Authorship serves as a poignant reminder that we hold the pen to our own life story. We possess the ability to script new plot twists at will, adapting the narrative of our lives to reflect our deepest desires and dreams. It is an empowering notion, emphasizing our infinite capacity to shape our experiences and manifest our true potential.

Celebrating the concept of finishing highlights our resilience and unwavering perseverance in the face of adversity. Life's challenges may test our resolve, but we have the innate ability to overcome obstacles, embodying the spirit of endurance. By acknowledging our strength and tenacity, we embrace the opportunity for growth and transformation that arises amidst life's trials.

As we explore these profound elements, we must recognize our own intrinsic value. Each of us is fearfully and wonderfully made, intricately designed with a unique purpose that fuels our daily breath. By shifting our perspective to align our actions, thoughts, and behavior with love, we embody the divine attributes we associate with God. This alignment empowers us to live a life that embraces love, compassion, and empathy, fostering positive connections and fostering a greater sense of harmony within ourselves and our communities.

In understanding these elements, we not only expand our perception of God, but we also unlock our own potential for growth and self-discovery. By recognizing the intimate connection between our own creative power and the divine, we can embark on a profound journey of personal empowerment and realize the transformative impact we can have on ourselves and the world around us.

Trinity: Spiritual Connections Rather than Magical Ideation

The concept of the Trinity, often surrounded by mysticism and seen as magical, can be better understood from a spiritual perspective. Rather than focusing on a mysterious phenomenon, we can explore the Trinity as a connected triad of Love, the example of how to relate and interact with love, and the indwelling of love that we can all embrace within ourselves.

At the core of this understanding is the recognition that our primary interaction is with ourselves. Cultivating self-love begins with speaking to ourselves with kindness and compassion. We set the stage for healthy relationships by understanding that love is not about being a doormat, but about valuing and respecting ourselves. By recognizing when mistreatment occurs and having the courage to let go when necessary, we honor ourselves and create space for genuine love to thrive.

Similarly, the indwelling of love is a spiritual give and take, even in moments of hope or when tangible things are not immediately evident. It is about making ourselves happy, cheering ourselves up, and finding our passion and purpose, even in solitude. The indwelling of love means nurturing our own emotional well-being and finding fulfillment within ourselves. It is a constant reminder that love is not solely dependent on external circumstances or the presence of another person.

By embracing the indwelling of love within ourselves, we tap into an infinite source of love that we can both give and receive. It is a recognition that love exists within us, independent of external factors. This understanding brings a sense of substance to our lives, even when tangible evidence may not be immediately visible. It allows us to cultivate joy, peace, and contentment from within, regardless of our external circumstances.

In the beautiful tapestry of life, we are each an integral part, and cultivating self-love is the thread that weaves us into the fabric of love's trinity. By nurturing our own well-being, practicing kindness and respect towards ourselves, and finding fulfillment within, we align ourselves with the indwelling of love. In this alignment, we create a strong foundation for healthy relationships with others and foster a deep connection with the spiritual essence of love itself.

So, let us approach the Trinity not as a magical concept, but as a spiritual connection. Let us recognize the power of our interactions with ourselves and embrace the indwelling of love within us. In doing so, we open ourselves to a profound and transformative journey of self-love and spiritual growth.

Beyond Self: Love—The Divine Image and Connection

When it comes to understanding our divine connection, we must comprehend that we were created in the image of love that extends beyond ourselves. We are manifestations of divine love—born from it, nurtured by it, and eventually returning to it.

The nature of love is to extend outside the self, to reach and touch others by transcending personal interests and desires. When we practice such love, we rise past the human ego and connect to our divine essence. We experience love not just as a fleeting emotion but as an inherent part of our identity—a potent sensation with a higher purpose.

When we love ourselves authentically and cultivate a strong foundation of self-love, we invite others to participate in what we create from that love. Our self-love becomes a conveyor and reflection of love itself, shining brightly and inspiring those around us to do the same.

As conduits of love, we transmit the essence of love through our thoughts, words, and actions. This is in alignment with the divine plan for us to become channels of love in the world. By emanating love, we reflect the beauty and power of God's essence, spreading love wherever we go.

Simultaneously, loving ourselves equips us with a remarkable capacity for compassion and empathy. When we embrace self-love, we recognize our own worth and value. We treat ourselves with kindness, understanding, and forgiveness. This same compassion and empathy that we offer ourselves naturally extend to others.

By giving ourselves love, we learn how to give love to others. We understand the importance of listening, supporting, and encouraging those around us. We become more attuned to their emotions and needs, fostering deeper connections and meaningful relationships.

This realization opens the door to performing 'miracles' in our everyday lives. Through our compassionate actions and empathetic presence, we have the power to positively impact the lives of others. Small acts of kindness, comforting words, and understanding gestures become transformative moments for those who receive them.

Furthermore, by loving ourselves and extending that love to others, we align ourselves with the divine plan for humanity. We become active participants in the universal flow of love. As we convey and reflect God's essence through our thoughts, words, and actions, we contribute to the collective healing and transformation of the world.

In this process, we also find a deeper connection with our creator. By embodying love and becoming channels of its expression, we draw closer to the divine source of all love. Our self-love becomes a path for us to return to our creator, deepening our spiritual journey and expanding our understanding of the interconnectedness of all beings.

So, let us embrace self-love and allow it to shine brightly, inviting others to participate in the love we create. By becoming conveyors and reflections of love, we align ourselves with the divine plan for humanity. Simultaneously, by loving ourselves, we equip ourselves with compassion and empathy, enabling us to perform extraordinary acts of love in our everyday lives. It is through this journey of love that we find our way back to the source and become channels of divine love in the world.

Chapter 11: Returning to God as Source

The Connection: Embodying Love and Power Through Connection

Rather than aiming for perfection, consider striving for a deep connection with the source of love—God. It is not our perfection that leads us on a divine path; rather, it is the connection to the source of love that enables us to channel divine power. By focusing on this connection, we invite God's love and power into our lives, which can empower us to do miracles and transform our worldview.

The Practice: Revisiting Adam, Eve, and Solomon's Temple

Understanding the practice of returning to God as the source requires looking at biblical stories such as that of Adam and Eve, as well as the structure of Solomon's temple.

- **The Tree of Good and Evil**: When Adam and Eve were commanded not to eat from the tree of good and evil, we learned to live our lives based on the dualism of good and evil. The decision to consume the fruit created a duality, rather than enjoying a non-dual experience rooted in connectivity with God. In the absence of this duality, everything becomes permissible as all actions stem from love, connection, and purpose.

- **Solomon's Temple**: The Temple's design holds significant symbolism. The most holy section was reserved for the high priest who was considered "pure" enough to enter God's presence, with a rope attached to his ankle as a safeguard. However, the Temple also had wings that, when folded, formed a cube. This structure provides access to all areas simultaneously, representing access beyond dualistic perspectives.

Dualism: Expanding the Human Story. In the majestic Garden of Eden, a perfect paradise, God created Adam and Eve, the first humans. They lived in harmony with nature, surrounded by beauty, and connected to their divine creator. But one cautionary command hovered over the garden: they were not to eat from the Tree of Good and Evil.

At first glance, this command may seem like a test of obedience or a simple restriction. However, its intention goes far beyond a mere prohibition. The essence of this command is not about keeping Adam and Eve from enjoying the physical fruits of the tree, but rather to safeguard them from a limited, dualistic existence.

The Tree of Good and Evil symbolizes the duality of life, the stark contrast between opposites. Eating from its fruit would grant Adam and Eve knowledge of good and evil, but it would also lead them down a path of judgment, separation, and moral absolutes. It would divide their experience into a rigid framework of right and wrong, black and white, without room for the vast spectrum of possibilities and interconnectedness.

By adhering to the command, Adam and Eve would have been able to transcend the dualistic mindset and embrace a non-dual existence rooted in connectivity with God and all creation. In this state of non-duality, every action and decision would stem from a place of love, connection, and purpose. They would be free from the constraints of moral judgments, as all deeds would be guided by their innate divine nature.

However, tempted by curiosity and enticed by the serpent, Adam and Eve succumbed to the forbidden fruit's allure. Instantly, their eyes were opened, and they became aware of good and evil. The consequence was not punishment inflicted by God, but a natural outcome of their choice. They had entered the realm of duality, where opposites clash and moral judgments arise.

From that moment, humanity's worldview became tainted by the dichotomy of good and evil. This dualistic perspective significantly influenced our understanding of right and wrong, shaping societies and belief systems throughout history. It led to moral codes, doctrines, and sometimes even wars fought over opposing ideologies.

Yet, hidden within the story of Adam and Eve is a profound message. It reminds us that the dualistic mindset is not the only way to perceive the world. We have the capacity to move beyond this limited perspective and embrace a non-dual existence, where love, connection, and purpose guide our actions.

Living in a non-dual state does not imply moral relativism or a lack of accountability. Rather, it invites us to see beyond the surface level of judgment and recognize the interconnectedness of all things. It encourages us to transcend the limitations of good and evil and approach life with love, compassion, and understanding.

The story of Adam and Eve and the Tree of Good and Evil serves as a timeless reminder that we have the choice to rise above dualistic thinking and embrace a non-dual existence. By doing so, we can reestablish our connection to the divine and live a life rooted in love, unity, and purpose.

Expanding the Temple Symbolism. The Temple of Solomon holds a crucial place in the history and culture of the Jewish and Christian traditions. Constructed in the 10th century BCE, it was a glorious structure that stood as a symbol of Israel's strength and prosperity. The temple consisted of several sections, but the most significant of them all was the "most holy place."

The most holy place was designed to be the inner sanctum of the temple, reserved only for the high priest, who was considered pure enough to enter God's presence. The room was separated from the other parts of the temple by a thick curtain, which represented the divide between the holiness of God and the world of mankind.

The high priest entered the most holy place only once a year, on the Day of Atonement, to seek God's forgiveness for the sins of the nation. This ritual symbolized the deep connection between humanity and divinity, with the high priest acting as a mediator between God and people.

The symbolism of the most holy place extends beyond the physical structure of the temple. The design of the temple as a whole is also rich with allegorical meaning. The wings of the temple, when folded, formed a perfect cube, representing access beyond dualistic perspectives.

In this way, the Temple offers an invitation to transcend the limited, dichotomous thinking that dominates our understanding of the world. It suggests that there is a way to access all areas simultaneously and to move beyond the either-or mentality that so often divides us.

The Temple of Solomon remains an enduring symbol of the relationship between humanity and divinity. Its design and function offer profound insights into our understanding of the world and our place within it. The temple also serves as a reminder of the possibilities of a non-dual existence. Rather than a linear approach with options right, left, forward, backward, the folded temple structure of the cube offers all options at once. It places you inside a box, but the box is not confining. It is a world of possibilities with access to the most holy place or the seat of decision making. You can choose happiness, success, and love as your birthright along the journey of life.

Non-Dual Possibilities: Expanding Perspectives and Aligning Vision

Divine love encompasses various facets that actively contribute to our self-development and growth. It goes beyond mere words and extends into action, verbal expression, thoughtful consideration, motivational growth, and inspirational perseverance.

First, active self-development demonstrates love through action. By intentionally engaging in self-care practices, such as nourishing meals or taking time to relax, we demonstrate our commitment and value for ourselves.

Verbal expression also plays a vital role in divine love. By articulating our intentions, affirmations, and aspirations, we give voice to our self-love. Whether spoken out loud or written down, verbalizing our love for ourselves makes it tangible and real.

Thoughtful self-love emphasizes understanding and capacity building. Engaging in mindfulness exercises, meditation, and moments of reflection nurtures our ability to truly comprehend ourselves and cultivate genuine love.

Motivational growth is another dimension of divine love. When faced with challenges and adversity, our resilience and continued prioritization of our well-being reveal the depth of our love. This growth under pressure shapes our character and showcases our commitment to self-love.

Lastly, inspirational perseverance fuels our self-development journey. It acts as a beacon of hope, encouraging us to persist even when progress seems uncertain. Drawing inspiration from external sources or tapping into our internal strength drives us towards nurturing deeper self-love.

Divine connection, within the context of divine love, is a profound invitation extended to others. It is an invitation to join, build, and be love in a way that surpasses individual capabilities. It acknowledges the power of collective love and the transformative potential it holds. It is an understanding that by coming together, sharing our love, and supporting one another, we can create something greater than what any of us could achieve alone. Divine connection calls us to transcend our individual boundaries and tap into a collective consciousness of love, fostering unity, growth, and the realization of our shared potential. You can engage this love and connection through as you embrace a non-dual, both-and approach to your journey.

To embrace non-dual possibilities, we can examine eight dimensions of self and others, both in our internal and external contexts (Social Influence, Social Agency, Interrelatedness, Self-Efficacy, Competence, Automation, and Acculturation). Imagine a cube with vertices on the inside and outside, symbolizing these dimensions in relation to personal evolution.

Each vertex represents a question to guide us in our growth and development:
1. Interior: How do we grow and develop as individuals in alignment with love and the choice we each hold?
2. Exterior: In what ways can we interact with the world to embody divine love and divine connection?

By exploring and reflecting on these questions, we can expand our understanding of ourselves and others, foster self-growth, and embrace non-dualistic perspectives.

We can mature and evolve by articulating a clear vision of our divine purpose and attracting experiences and connections through these sixteen dimensions of love. Through love, we create a new reality that transcends traditional dualistic ideas of good and evil, allowing us to live in harmony with others and flourish as divine beings.

Chapter 12: Love from Abundance

Love as Infinite Source: Rewriting Your Story

When we recognize that love is an infinite source that resides within us, we can rewrite our story and transform our perception of love. Instead of seeking external validation or love from others, we shift our focus to expressing love generously and unconditionally, stemming from a sense of abundance within.

Embodying love in this way transports us to the spiritual plane, where we can experience the presence of the divine. In this realm, love is whole and complete, resources are boundless, and limitless possibilities are within our grasp. As we deepen our connection with this infinite source of love, it begins to flow through us, filling us with a sense of inner healing and leading to its manifestation in our lives.

By tapping into the infinite source of love, we rewrite the narrative that suggests love is scarce or dependent on others. We understand that love is not something we acquire or seek externally, but a wellspring that originated within our own being. This awareness liberates us from the limitations of conditional and transactional love, enabling us to love freely, authentically, and abundantly.

As we embrace the essence of love as an infinite source, our inner abundance overflows, shaping our relationships, experiences, and growth. We become conduits of love, radiating its transformative power into the world around us. This profound shift in perspective liberates us from the confines of fear, self-doubt, and ego-driven desires, propelling us toward a path of compassion, empathy, and unity.

Through our connection with the divine source of love, we become active participants in co-creating a reality where love is the guiding force. We recognize that our capacity to love is limitless, and we are empowered to extend this love to others, fostering a collective evolution towards a more harmonious and compassionate existence.

But this journey requires intention, practice, and self-awareness. It necessitates letting go of old narratives that have limited our understanding of love and cultivating a deep-rooted belief in our own worthiness of love and the ability to express it abundantly.

In rewriting our story, we embrace the truth that we are beings of love, interconnected in a vast web of divine energy. As we tap into this wellspring, we not only nourish our own souls but also inspire and uplift others, creating a ripple effect of love and transformation.

Love Begins with Self: Balancing Love and Self-Respect

Love is not solely a force that impacts our relationships with others but begins with ourselves. It is through self-love that we experience transformative growth, self-discovery, and acceptance. To nurture love within ourselves, we must prioritize self-care, self-awareness, and self-respect.

Self-care is essential in nurturing love within ourselves. Taking time for activities that bring us joy, physical and emotional well-being, and relaxation allows us to replenish and recharge. By prioritizing our own needs, we demonstrate to ourselves that we are deserving of love and care.

Self-awareness plays a crucial role in cultivating self-love. By exploring our thoughts, emotions, and patterns of behavior, we gain a deeper understanding of ourselves. Embracing our feelings and emotions as valid and honest expressions of our experiences allows us to embrace our whole selves, including any perceived flaws or vulnerabilities.

Additionally, surrendering our burdens and challenges to the divine power of love allows us to release negativity and renew our perspective each day. This act of surrendering reminds us that we are not alone in our journey and that divine love is always available to support us.

Alongside nurturing self-love, love acts as a counterbalance against abuse, mistreatment, and disrespect. When we cultivate a strong foundation of self-esteem through self-love, we empower ourselves to set healthy boundaries with others. We recognize that our well-being should never be compromised or subjected to mistreatment.

By prioritizing self-respect, we create a filter through which we evaluate and engage with others. We become attuned to recognizing when actions or words disrespect our boundaries or compromise our well-being. Self-respect allows us to honor our worth and seek relationships that align with this understanding.

Balancing love and self-respect also involve maintaining authenticity and integrity in our interactions. It means expressing ourselves honestly and truthfully, without compromising our values or sacrificing our own needs for the sake of others. This authenticity strengthens our relationships and ensures that love is reciprocated in healthy and respectful ways.

Active Creation: Love as a Lifestyle

Love is not a passive force that we wait for or wish to happen to us. Instead, we can actively create an environment where love thrives. This shift in approach involves embracing the spiritual plane of existence, where love energy magnetizes like energy, fostering an abundance of genuine and unreserved love.

The concept of magnetic love refers to the idea that love attracts love. When we embody and express love, we attract those who resonate with this energy and are similarly inclined to reciprocate love. This allows us to form healthy and fulfilling relationships where love flows effortlessly.

Creating an environment where love thrives begins with cultivating love as an integral part of our daily practices. This involves understanding and embracing the complexity of our human experience. It means accepting and honoring the contradictions, nuances, and complexities that define us, allowing space for vulnerability, strength, fear, and courage to coexist within our psyche.

By accepting our intricacies as human beings, we open ourselves up to experiencing love in its many forms. We become more attuned to our emotions and are better equipped to communicate our feelings to others. As a result, we form deeper and more fulfilling connections with ourselves and those around us.

Cultivating love as a lifestyle also involves being intentional in our interactions and relationships. It means actively seeking out opportunities to express love and compassion in our daily lives. This could involve performing acts of kindness towards friends, colleagues, or strangers, or making time to connect meaningfully with loved ones.

Additionally, love as a lifestyle means prioritizing our own growth and self-care. This could involve engaging in activities that bring us joy and fulfillment, such as pursuing a hobby or spending time in nature. It also means prioritizing our physical and emotional health and seeking support when necessary.

By making love a lifestyle, we prioritize relationships that align with our values and beliefs. We form deeper and more meaningful connections with others and create a community of love and support.

This shift in approach allows us to live authentically and purposefully and fosters a sense of fulfillment and joy in our lives.

Navigating Challenges: Acceptance, Resilience, and Courage

When we embrace authentic self-acceptance and make love a part of our daily practice, we inevitably encounter challenges along the way. However, we can navigate these challenges with resilience, self-understanding, and self-compassion. By returning to the source of love regularly and offering ourselves grace, we allow our feelings to flow without judgment.

Navigating challenges begins with self-acceptance. It involves recognizing and accepting ourselves as imperfect beings with flaws, doubts, fears, and vulnerabilities. When we approach our challenges with self-acceptance, we shift our perspective from self-criticism to self-compassion. We acknowledge that it is natural to face setbacks and difficulties and learn to treat ourselves with kindness and understanding during these times.

Resilience plays a critical role in navigating challenges. It is the ability to bounce back from adversity, setbacks, or disappointments. Cultivating resilience involves developing a growth mindset and viewing challenges as opportunities for learning and growth. Rather than viewing failures as permanent, we see them as steppingstones on our journey towards self-improvement. Resilience empowers us to persevere through challenges, face them head-on, and emerge stronger and wiser on the other side.

Self-understanding is another key element in navigating challenges. It involves deepening our understanding of ourselves, our patterns, and our triggers. By exploring our emotions, thoughts, and reactions with curiosity, we gain insight into our inner world. This self-awareness enables us to recognize the root causes of our challenges, allowing us to address them effectively and make conscious choices aligned with our values.

Courage is essential in navigating challenges because it requires us to step out of our comfort zone and face difficult situations head-on. It is through courage that we push past our fears and doubts and take the necessary steps towards growth and transformation. By embracing courage, we expand our capacity to overcome challenges and embrace new opportunities for love and growth.

When we navigate challenges with self-acceptance, resilience, self-understanding, and courage, we emerge from the turmoil stronger, wiser, and better equipped to handle future challenges. Each time we dive into our inner world and befriend our doubts, fears, and vulnerabilities, we gain valuable insights and lessons. These experiences shape us and help us develop a greater sense of self-awareness and emotional intelligence.

Additionally, navigating challenges teaches us the importance of building robust relationships. As we face and overcome challenges, we grow as individuals, making us better equipped to navigate the complexities of relationships. We develop deeper empathy, patience, and understanding towards others, fostering stronger and more authentic connections. By embracing our own challenges and supporting others in navigating their own, we create a community rooted in love, compassion, and mutual growth.

From Abundance: Cultivating an Unlimited Store of Love

Loving ourselves sets the foundation for an unlimited supply of love. This boundless reserve is generated continuously as we reflect and appreciate every aspect of our journey—our abilities, progress, experiences, and even our pain. Both the peaks and valleys of life contribute to our growth, our 'becoming', and are worthy of love.

The practice of self-reflection, especially on our determination to keep moving forward despite challenges, can significantly amplify our capacity to love. This overflowing love naturally extends to others, enhancing our relationships and reinforcing our empathetic connections.

One of the key realizations in this journey is that love, when it spills over from abundance, is never wasted. Be it received, reciprocated, or merely felt, it only adds to the beauty and richness of our lives. The act of loving—both ourselves and others—becomes an effortless, fulfilling, and deeply rewarding experience.

Thus, when we practice self-love, acknowledge our journey, and appreciate our becoming, we inherently cultivate a love that knows no boundaries—one that overflows naturally and abundantly into every facet of our lives.

Love Is by Dr. Michael A. Wright

(Patience) *Patience embraces everything in its time. Patience is the capacity and the willingness to accept delay, difficulty, or annoyance without becoming angry or upset. Given to self, it feels like grace and progress at a steady pace.*

(Kindness) *Kindness considers the capacity of the giver rather than holding unreasonable expectations. Kindness to oneself is treating ourselves with compassion and understanding, the same way we would treat a loved one. It's accepting our faults and mistakes and replacing self-criticism and judgement with self-nurture and care.*

(Forgiveness) *Forgiveness takes responsibility without listing an account of all the wrongs. Self-forgiveness is about letting go of guilt and resentment towards oneself for past mistakes while remaining accountable for learning and more sustainable choices.*

(Humility) *Humility is the mindful recognition of our limitations and acceptance of our flaws. It also includes celebrating our strengths without arrogance. Implementing humility in self-love means* acknowledging that we have areas for growth and being willing to learn from our mistakes instead of condemning ourselves for them.

(Honor) Honor refers to treating yourself with respect and integrity. It means being true to your values and principles, standing by them even when you're standing alone. By implementing honor in self-love, you show yourself the same level of respect and care that you would give to others, treating your feelings, thoughts, and experiences as valid and worthwhile.

(Civility) Civility involves being polite and respectful in your behavior and attitude towards yourself. As part of self-love, being civil to yourself means treating yourself kindly, especially during moments of mistakes or failures.

(Consideration) Consideration in self-love entails being mindful of your needs—physically, mentally, and emotionally. Give thought to your actions in the context of authentic reflections and consider their potential impact on choices and the resulting well-being.

(Temperance) Temperance is the ability to maintain balance, moderation, and self-restraint. In self-love, it means making choices that foster long-term health and happiness, even when those choices demand patience and self-control.

(Generosity) Generosity in self-love isn't about giving material things to yourself. It's more about being generous with patience, understanding, and forgiveness towards yourself.

(Honesty) *Honesty begins with truly understanding and embracing your feelings, emotions, strengths, and weaknesses. Living in your truth empowers you to stand confidently as you make your choices in life.*

(Protection) *Protection ensures that you safeguard your mental and emotional health from negativity and harm. This is not immediate isolation or blocking. It is setting your filter and discernment to process interactions objectively.*

(Reason) *Reason encourages you to adopt a rational approach towards your self-perceptions and self-judgment. As self-love, this looks like accepting and tracing your motivations with respect and attentiveness.*

(Trust) *Trusting involves believing in your own abilities and potentials, building faith in yourself to take control of your destiny, and fostering a consistent, disciplined choice routine toward sustainability.*

(Hopefulness) *Visualize a brighter future regardless of the current challenges and maintain a hopeful attitude to nourish your dreams.*

(Perseverance) *Investing the time, dedication, and unwavering determination to learn, practice, and grow and achieve remarkable growth.*

www.ingramcontent.com/pod-product-compliance
Lightning Source LLC
Chambersburg PA
CBHW060326050426
42449CB00011B/2665